THE MIND OF DANTE

THE MIND OF
DANTE

EDITED BY

U. LIMENTANI

*Professor of Italian in the
University of Cambridge*

CAMBRIDGE
AT THE UNIVERSITY PRESS
1965

PUBLISHED BY
THE SYNDICS OF THE CAMBRIDGE UNIVERSITY PRESS

Bentley House, 200 Euston Road, London, N.W. 1
American Branch: 32 East 57th Street, New York, N.Y. 10022
West African Office: P.O. Box 33, Ibadan, Nigeria

©

CAMBRIDGE UNIVERSITY PRESS

1965

Printed in Great Britain at the University Printing House, Cambridge
(Brooke Crutchley, University Printer)

LIBRARY OF CONGRESS CATALOGUE
CARD NUMBER: 65-21790

CONTENTS

v

FOREWORD

The seven essays that are collected in this volume reproduce, with some slight differences in detail, the text of
the lectures that were delivered in the University of
Cambridge during the Lent Term, 1965, to mark the
seventh centenary of the birth of Dante.

The opening lecture by Natalino Sapegno was given
in Italian; it has been translated into English by P.
Boyde. The other six essays are by members of the
Department of Italian in the University of Cambridge,
and each one of them is meant to illustrate an aspect of
the poetry or of the thought of Dante. It is hoped that
they will serve as an introduction to his works, and as an
interpretation of his art and ideas.

U. L

Cambridge
March 1965

The text used in quoting from and in referring to Dante's works is *Le opere di Dante*—Testo critico della Società Dantesca Italiana (Florence, 1921 and repr. 1960)

GENESIS AND STRUCTURE:
TWO APPROACHES TO
THE POETRY OF THE 'COMEDY'

NATALINO SAPEGNO

It was in 1921 that Benedetto Croce[1] drew the distinction between 'poetry' and 'structure' in the *Comedy*, and we shall not be risking too great a simplification if we say that all subsequent criticism of the poem has taken this distinction as its point of departure, and found in it a fertile stimulus to discussion. It is true that today some critics are inclined to deny all validity to the solution which Croce proposed. But even they agree, and will continue to agree, that its formulation was a major land-mark in the evolution of Dante criticism, a point of ex-ceptionally lucid self-awareness; and this notwithstanding the danger it undoubtedly brought of a one-sided and distorted reading of Dante's text.

It is of course true that Croce's thesis was far from being a discovery *ex nihilo*—an entirely new criterion of inter-pretation born suddenly and quite spontaneously from the brain of a philosopher. He himself intended it as the re-duction to exact logical terms of an attitude to Dante, and an approach to his work, that has its antecedents in a centuries-old tradition. To this tradition we can relate—

[1] B. Croce, *La poesia di Dante* (Bari, G. Laterza, 1921). See p. 31, n. 1.

making due allowances for the different cultural situations—the caution and diffidence with which Renaissance men of letters approached a poem which, as regards both its conceptual content and its expressive means, was so utterly unlike the ideas about poetry and art which they upheld in theory and in practice. To it also belong the distaste, indifference and aloofness shown by readers of the Arcadian school and throughout the ages of the Enlightenment and Neoclassicism, who were no less repelled by Dante's scholasticism and a style which seemed an affront to sane and civilized good taste in its entire lack of restraint. And to the same tradition belong even those first attempts by early nineteenth-century critics in Germany, England, France and Italy to formulate a distinction, and thereby a dialectical definition, of the various and contradictory elements in the work. In the history of Dante criticism there is a constant and coherent line of development which runs from the admiration tempered with doubts that are not merely linguistic shown by Bembo: to Voltaire's antipathy; to the fastidious choice of a Bettinelli, torn between his admiration of the genius, and his condemnation of an archaic and turbid taste; to Vico's discovery of the 'primitive Dante', the new Homer, under the unseemly and repellent cloak of the scholastic philosopher; to the contrast, made in the work of Schlegel and Bouterweck, between those elements in the poem which derive from a perishable culture and those which are the imaginative representation of man and the supernatural. (Bouterweck indeed recommended that the *Comedy* should be read in episodes, in fragments—*frag-*

mentarisch schätzen.) It is true that each critic in turn forged the critical method best adapted to the kind and degree of his philosophical formation, but in each case this was only to re-emphasize their consciousness that it was impossible to accept Dante's poem in its entirety, impossible to assimilate the massive and undigested complexity of this single organic entity.

The story of this era of Dante criticism—which began early and continued in various forms for hundreds of years—was, then, one of failure to understand, or at least of rather hostile mistrust of a book of unusual character, which was in sharp conflict with later taste: a taste which evolved, but which was substantially homogeneous, and was still present in the Romantics, notwithstanding their genuine concern to understand Dante, and their rather one-sided and ingenuous cult of the Middle Ages.

Croce picked up the thread of this tradition of reading Dante with detachment and reservations, beset with doubts, rejections or only partial acceptances. But he made no attempt to resolve it in a way that would permit a less blinkered historical vision, one which would take more account of the specific cultural characteristics of a given epoch or author. Quite the contrary in fact: because, fundamentally, Croce accepted the basic assumption of the tradition that the *Comedy* was an extremely heterogeneous work and, in many of its parts, unpoetic. And far from demolishing the contradictions latent in that critical position, his aim was rather to rationalize it, to translate it into a logical formula that was truly appropriate and convincing. Dante, he says—and readers of the

Romantic age, or even Bembo or Bettinelli, would all have endorsed his opinion—Dante was without doubt a poetic genius, and the poetic material of his book is great and wide-ranging. (Here we must give Croce credit for having greatly extended the scope of such a 'poetic reading', applying it to areas that before him had remained unnoticed or had not been widely understood.) But, he goes on, the poetry does not lie in the foundations of the work itself. It is grafted on to the purely intellectual architecture of a 'theological novel', which is constructed in view of ends which are political, moralistic and polemical. And if we are to feel and really understand Dante the poet, in all his varied, rich, unpredictable and at times even self-contradictory humanity, then we not only *can* but *must* set that novel on one side. For Dante's true feelings are expressed time and again in the poem quite independently of—and sometimes in clear contradiction to—the requirements of its narrative and doctrinal structure, requirements which have nothing to do with poetry and in any case have very little interest for a modern reader.

Within the limits of the critical tradition outlined above, Croce's solution is logically unobjectionable, and it has its uses as a counter-weight to the sentimental and indiscriminate admiration of the poem, shown by literary people and scholars alike, which was so prevalent when Croce's book appeared. It has the merit of refocusing our attention on the aesthetic properties of the *Comedy*, which are not necessarily to be identified with the pattern of ideas imposed by an outdated ideology—ethical, political and religious—nor with a particular historical phase of human life and thought. Moreover, his solution finds its place in a wider system of ideas, inasmuch as it exhibits in the particular case of Dante the polarity of 'poetry' and 'structure' which is to be found, as Croce recognized, in every work of art. For no work of art can ever be completely reduced to a 'lyrical state of feeling'; each takes effect as a poetic motif realized in terms which are to some extent rational and logical. The only difference in the *Comedy* is that here the rational element is so powerfully evident that there is no possibility of ignoring it, as there may be in works of lesser proportions or, in any case, of a structure less profoundly conceived and less majestically articulated. In this sense Croce's thesis is a universal philosophical hypothesis, and one to be regarded with respect. It can lead the way to a new and deeper analysis of the logical components of a work of art, an analysis which should render it possible to arrive at conclusions which would markedly differ from those of Croce, and would in fact represent an advance with respect to his own system.

And yet what happened when Croce's book was published is well known. Very few of its first readers were disposed to accept, whether in whole or in part, the critical criterion he put forward. In many cases the rejection was due to nothing but that aura of admiration and almost of worship which often surrounds exceptional personalities, especially those who are considered representative of the spirit of a nation. But in the best critics the rejection proceeded from a feeling that a deeper and more subtle approach was required, one which would do more justice to the impression which an unprejudiced reader receives from the *Comedy* of a profound unity of conception and artistic expression.

There is no need here to examine the validity of the reasons given by these first opponents of Croce to justify their disagreement with him (more often than not they argued in a manner that was far from happy, accepting all too passively the abstract formulation of the problem). It is more to the point to stress the fact that while Dante criticism after 1921 began with these purely theoretical discussions of Croce's ideas, it has since developed more independently and has consciously departed from Croce in order to explore new and more fruitful paths.

It is a fact that in our day conditions are perhaps more favourable for the study of the *Comedy* than ever before. We are able to approach the work with a greater willingness to understand its nature and essence, and to overcome that attitude of incomprehension or—what comes to the same thing—partial or fragmentary comprehension which characterized all earlier criticism. Only in our day, I would say, has it become possible to offer a rational justification of the admiration manifested down the centuries—an admiration that was always confused and always open to objections, that was affirmed rather than genuinely felt, and formulated in the vaguest and most incongruous terms. Today we approach the evaluation of the medieval heritage without bias. This is possible for two reasons. On the one hand we have repudiated all polemical attitudes derived from Humanism, the Renaissance, the Enlightenment or even from Romanticism. On the other we now have a thoroughly mature historical sense. The historical point of view has become almost second nature to us, enabling us to approach each and every phase in human history with a complete lack of prejudice, an entire freedom from inhibitions, a readiness simply to understand. This is to say that our attitude to the past has become strictly intellectual and impartial, but at the same time infinitely curious, infinitely sensitive to all manifestations of human nature in space and time.

So far as Dante is concerned, this new historical sense has been nourished by a very great increase in our knowledge of medieval culture. We have the advantage over our predecessors of a far wider, richer and more subtle understanding of the history, institutions and spiritual problems of the Middle Ages. And all this new knowledge is the necessary precondition of any reading of the *Comedy* that is to be really close—never generic and vague, always attentive to every detail of the text; the kind of reading, indeed, of which Dante's first commentators in the fourteenth century offer a permanent example. And it is their work, in fact, which we are now in a position to take up and continue. We have found our way back to the path which they were following and which their immediate successors lost. For, despite a certain ingenuousness, those early commentators were essentially on the right lines: they had no axe to grind and they interpreted Dante's poetry by methods that were in harmony with its spirit.

The essential foundations of this new approach to the study of history were laid—in an inchoate and premonitory way—by the philosophers and critics of the Romantic movement, even though they were still steeped in preconceptions inherited from the Renaissance and the Enlightenment. And so it comes as no surprise that, in the pages of these same philosophers and critics, we can discern the first traces of the new Dante criticism which prevails today. In many different ways, here more clearly and there less so, we can see that they all tended to the view that the central critical problem was that of how the *Comedy* was to be read as a unified whole, set in the context of a specific historical and cultural situation: this was the approach, for example, of Hegel and De Sanctis. It is true that Croce was inclined to see these two critics, not as the first to break with the critical tradition to which he himself gave definitive and final form, but as the confused precursors of his own thesis. But this was only the consequence of his rather arbitrary and distorted exposition of their ideas, as we shall see more clearly by dwelling a little on the views of De Sanctis,[1] the man who of all the great Romantic critics most deserves a place in the kind of broad survey of Dante criticism attempted here.

It was Croce who first called attention to the fact that all De Sanctis's criticism of the *Comedy*, at every period in his career, centred on the crucial problem of the duality of theological system and poetic invention, of the 'structure' and the 'poetry'; or, in other words, that De Sanctis saw the problem in the terms one would expect of someone who followed in the wake of Romantic criticism (Bouterweck, Schlegel) and of the profound elaborations in aesthetic theory made after Kant (Hegel, Schelling).

---

[1] F. De Sanctis, *Lezioni e saggi su Dante*, ed. S. Romagnoli (Torino, Einaudi, 1955).

Similarly, it was Croce who pointed to the uncertainty and ambiguity of the successive formulae which De Sanctis used in this connexion: now contrasting 'allegory' and 'poetry'; now trying to interpret the complex relations between 'heaven' and 'earth'; finally investigating the transition from what he called the 'world of *intention*' to the 'world of *art*'. Since Croce was to end by making a distinction, and, to some extent, an opposition between 'poetry' and 'structure' (= non-poetry), it was only natural that he should have given particular prominence in his diagnosis to De Sanctis's uncertainty and ambiguity on this point. But what Croce failed to see was precisely what justified the many years of intensive thought that De Sanctis devoted to this unresolved problem, to which he returned again and again from different angles and with formulae now more and now less penetrating; as it is also what explains the relevance of his work today, viewed outside the terms of Croce's coherent but facile and evasive solution. What Croce failed to see was that De Sanctis posed the problem of the duality (or, as we should say, the complexity) of the *Comedy not in terms of a 'distinction', still less of an 'opposition', but in terms of a 'relationship'*. In other words, he placed the emphasis on the need to re-establish—though not by reducing to unity the factors involved, but rather by correlating them dialectically—the unity of the *Comedy* as a work of poetry.

Just how far De Sanctis's thought on this matter evolved, we may demonstrate by contrasting its extreme terms. At the beginning we have the lectures given in Naples in 1842-3. There the problem is posed, in formulae that are still strictly Hegelian, as the encounter of a 'divine idea' and 'human form'; and the unifying element is seen mainly in the constant presence of Dante the protagonist. At the end we have the famous fourth lecture given in Zürich in 1856. Here, through a rigorous critique of Hegel's aesthetic, De Sanctis transcends any distinction between idea and form, and form is apprehended as an organic unity embracing the total content viewed from a strictly aesthetic standpoint. We need not here consider the importance of these conclusions for the elaboration of a general theory or methodology. The point to establish is that it was along just this road that De Sanctis found it possible to reach a deeper and more satisfying solution to his specific problem.

De Sanctis was never really able to find one firm point where he could resolve all the contradictions that arose from his different analytical procedures: whenever he seemed to have found it, it proved only a temporary solution. He adopted several distinct positions, but these do not follow one another in a clear line of development: they alternate, they overlap, they are in part contradictory. Nevertheless, provided these qualifications are kept in mind, the following rather schematic outline of his dialectic will be found substantially accurate.

When construction and invention in the *Comedy* presented themselves to him as a political and religious ideology in allegorical dress, he saw the relationship between allegory and poetry as an absurd attempt, rooted in a medieval and scholastic mentality, to reconcile two conflicting elements which were *a priori* irreconcilable.

But the kind of allegorical transference performed by the abstractive intellect is scarcely to be found anywhere in the *Comedy*. And a closer, deeper reading of the text led him to adopt a formula which reflected more faithfully the way in which Dante's invention really took shape. When he defined that invention as the encounter of this world and the next, of earth and heaven, then the cleavage which he had affirmed so inflexibly was narrowed and largely closed. His humanistic sensibility and certain of his Romantic predilections—formed on the archetypes of Shakespeare and Schiller—may have led him to equate the poetic values of the *Comedy* with the reality and experience of *this* world. But he was well aware that the *other* world was no mere accessory in Dante, but rather a stimulus: a stimulus that worked at the very heart of his conception of reality, and which was capable of modifying that conception from within, conferring on it new and richer dimensions. And so he became aware that the two worlds are, at every point, 'omnipresent and reciprocal'; that

they succeed and alternate with each other, cross and compenetrate, explain and illuminate each other in constant interaction. Their unity does not lie in a protagonist, nor in a dramatic action, nor in an abstract goal extraneous to the subject-matter. It is in this subject-matter itself—an inner, non-personal unity, a living, indivisible, organic unity, the elements of which do not follow each other in the poet's mind as a necessary aggregate of divisible parts, but penetrate each other and combine just as in life.

When De Sanctis perceived that the object of Dante's poetry was none other than 'human life seen from the other world', and that, conversely, because of the changed perspective, people and events take on 'another face' in his poetry, 'because they appear to us on the pedestal of infinity', then he came very near to laying his finger on the crux of the problem. But he did not rest even in this position, nor was he able to develop it to the full.

When, finally, he fell back on his formula of a 'world of intention' and a 'world of poetry', he again became aware of a contradiction between the two planes. But at the same time he felt the need to establish a bridge between them, by which the one—the abstract content—would realize itself in the other, becoming concrete as it merged and combined with that form. Thus, not only did he perceive intuitively the unity of the two dimensions—those of this world and the next—but he devised an interpretative principle able to seize that unity as it took shape. The problem of evaluating the poetry resolved itself into that of how a narrative of biographical and intellectual reality became poetry when reflected in the fire of an individual experience.

It must be remembered that the different positions in De Sanctis's dialectic have here been distinguished only schematically. They are not the phases of an ordered and progressively deeper investigation of the problem, but rather the alternating positions, the wavering and contradictory attempts to solve a difficult problem to which he never found the solution, and to which he therefore returned again and again. But what is important is that at all times De Sanctis felt the need to affirm the poetic unity of the *Comedy*, and this not by rejecting its structural and doctrinal components, but by accepting and reabsorbing them. Far from being a precursor of Croce's disciples in their purely sophistic disputations on the relationship between poetry and structure, De Sanctis took as his very point of departure the need to experience the meaning of the poem as a whole and not in episodes. And he found a formula to define the poem which is perhaps the most apt, and certainly one of the most dense, of the many that critics have devised. He proposed to call it 'the poem of the Universe, the eternal geometry and the eternal logic of creation incarnated in the three worlds of Christianity: the city of God in which is reflected the city of man in all the reality of a particular time and place, the one being the type, exemplar and judge of the other'.

And it is not less important that the kind of solution towards which De Sanctis was feeling his way—however uncertainly—lay in a study of the *genesis* of the *Comedy*: that is, in the reconstruction of the psychological, historical and cultural factors which influenced the act of imaginative creation, Dante's elaboration of his myth of the other world. In this respect the pages of his *History of Italian Literature* which trace the formation of the poet's personality, showing the successive layers of experience and culture, may be regarded as the goal of his long endeavours—a goal still insufficient, but important none the less. These pages map a path that is still essential for scholars even today, especially in so far as they stress the fundamental and central importance, in Dante's experience, of his exile from Florence, and of the meditation on politics provoked by that crisis.

What were the main obstacles which prevented De Sanctis from pursuing his inquiry to a successful conclusion, and, more important, from applying his principles consistently to the analysis of the text? First, there was his strongly Romantic sensibility, which made it impossible for him to respond with sympathy to the themes and forms of medieval poetics, and which also explains his dislike not just of allegorical interpretation, but of any kind of symbolical interpretation in however broad a sense. Second, and perhaps more important, he still clung to certain attitudes inherited from the Enlightenment, which prevented him from understanding or making any positive evaluation of Dante's 'world of intention'—his religious culture and his scholastic modes of thought. These same attitudes account for his persistent deafness to certain registers of Dante's poetry, especially in the *Paradiso*. And they also explain why—even in those parts of the poem which were most accessible to his taste (for example, in the episodes of Francesca and Farinata)—he gave quite inadequate attention to the moral and theological tensions which determine the complexity and the drama of the great myths in the *Comedy*.

This is not the moment to examine one by one the stages in the evolution of Dante criticism from De Sanctis to the present day, nor even to recall the more important suggestions put forward by scholars in an effort to transcend the limitations of De Sanctis's interpretation, while still remaining faithful—often unconsciously—to his fundamental premisses. There are many roads by which one may penetrate to the heart of Dante's poetry in the *Comedy*, and they differ greatly from one another in their method and in their aims. Each can be useful to some degree, provided we recognize that each has its limits, and that each needs to be complemented by the others. In this way, the technical analyses of the linguist and the philosopher, the contributions of the philologist and the historian, the impressions of the poetry-lover can finally come together in a harmonious description in which all are absorbed and justified. It is significant, however, that we feel increasingly impelled to try to piece together a complete picture of Dante's life and culture in the period when the *Comedy* was born, in order that the purely abstract problem of the 'structure' of the fictional 'theological novel' may be resolved into that of its 'genesis'. For it was the actual 'genesis' of the work which fixed at once its subject-matter, its logical architecture, its structure, the free and wide-ranging role of imagination, the novelty and wealth of the expressive resources. The *Comedy* is first and foremost the whole of Dante's life, both emotional and intellectual. But as well as being the expression of its author's personality, the poem crowns and epitomizes a great period in the history of civilization. That period is caught in its final phase, on the very brink of disintegration, and this is why it is portrayed in such passionate, emotive and dramatic colours. This, too, is why Dante chose poetry as his vehicle rather than the—theoretically possible—treatise or sermon.

One will probably be forced to abandon not merely certain of Croce's critical opinions but his entire system if one is to adopt the kind of critical position we have outlined—in which poetry is no longer conceived as existing in timeless categories, and in which it is recognized that the form and essence of each work of poetry are always determined in strict relation to the history and culture of the period in which it was born. However, it is more fitting to close on a positive note by emphasizing that it was De Sanctis who first indicated the task which awaits Dante criticism today—a task which we are better equipped to carry out now that we are free from the prejudices he inherited from the Enlightenment and Romanticism, and now that we have access to fuller and more accurate scholarship. That task is to deepen our knowledge of the 'genesis' of Dante's poem until we reach the desired point where we can make our understanding of the structure—analysed and dissected in its every detail—coincide with our total discovery of the poetry.

THE POETRY OF THE
'COMEDY'

PHILIP McNAIR

For most civilized people, the *Comedy* is the greatest poem ever written. Shakespeare was Dante's peer, but never wrote one work which attempted and achieved so much. The greatness of the *Comedy* is seen in the attempt as well as in the achievement, for whether he succeeds or fails, by any human standard its author has engaged in an enormous enterprise. If he succeeds, his success is Olympian; if he fails, his failure is Titanic. Even if we think that his poem reveals a chaotic mind (and, incredible as it seems, there have been critics who thought this), at least we should concede that it is the chaos of a great mind. But it is because the poet has succeeded with incomparable success that Dante's name is honoured the world over in this seventh centenary of his birth.

We honour Dante first and foremost as a poet, yet the *Comedy* is not primarily a poem but something else which is rather more difficult to define. The poetry is incidental to some purpose, a means toward some end. The Anglican liturgy is not primarily sonorous and rhythmic prose but a vehicle of worship, and if we stop short at the prose we shall remain men of letters and not men of God. Isaiah was not primarily writing poetry but prophecy, although the prophetic word is mediated through the poet's image;

if we enjoy the imagery and ignore the prophecy, the prophet would have called us dull of sight and hard of hearing and denounced us as idolaters. That fashion of the 1930's which gave us *The Bible Designed to be Read as Literature* did not last because the Bible was designed to be read as the Bible. It is great literature, of course, but it is more than literature, and even as literature it fails if it is only literature and not food for our souls, a lamp unto our feet. In popular jargon, it has a 'message'. A child will hold a hand-grenade to his ear and chuckle at its ticking: so Shelley read his Bible daily to revel in its poetry. But the poetry is only effective poetry if it conveys the message —if the terror makes us afraid, and the glory makes us glad. In the same way (having due regard to the qualitative difference between God's Word and Man's) there is more to Dante's poem than the poetry. The poet is conscious of a mission to a world astray, and his high purpose is for ever sounding through his verse. In the wise words of a distinguished American scholar: 'The *Comedy* is the greatest of all poems, yet it is only secondarily a poem: it is primarily an instrument of salvation.'[1]

The instrument which Dante forged for the world's salvation is an allegory of God, Man and the Devil, set in the three-storeyed Universe of medieval Catholic belief; and although my concern is with the poetry of the *Comedy* rather than its 'message', it is important to define what kind of allegory he intended to write, and what relation the allegory bears to the poetry. Dante himself has left us

---

[1] Ernest H. Wilkins, *A History of Italian Literature* (Harvard University Press, Cambridge, Mass., 1954), p. 61.

three or four clues which, taken together, raise a critical problem. In his *Convivio* he interprets one of his own love-poems according to what he calls the allegory of poets as distinct from the allegory of theologians, and has this to say about the distinction:

Literature can be understood and should be expounded in four main senses. The first is called literal, and this is the sense which does not go beyond the letter of the fictional words in which poets tell their fables. The second is called allegorical, and this is the sense which is concealed beneath the cloak of such fables, and is a truth hidden under a beautiful fiction ['una veritade ascosa sotto bella menzogna']; as when Ovid says that Orpheus with his lyre made wild animals tame and moved trees and stones towards him, which means that the wise man softens and humbles cruel hearts by the instrument of his voice, and moves at his will those who live neither for science nor art [...] It is true that theologians take this sense differently from poets, but since I intend here to follow the method of poets, I shall take the allegorical sense according to their usage. (*Con.* II, i, 2–4.)

In other words, the literal sense of poet's allegory is fictive and subserves the hidden meaning, whereas the literal sense of theologian's allegory is veridical and exists in its own right. Dante's distinction is in fact between allegory and symbolism, and it has been well said that 'symbolism is a mode of thought, but allegory is a mode of expression'.[1]

On the only two occasions in the *Comedy* when Dante calls our attention to the fact that he is writing allegory, it is to poet's and not theologian's allegory that he points. After a curious passage in the *Inferno* about the Furies and Medusa we read:

[1] C. S. Lewis, *The Allegory of Love* (Clarendon Press, Oxford, 1936), p. 48.

2-2

O voi ch'avete li 'ntelletti sani,
   mirate la dottrina che s'asconde
   sotto i velame de li versi strani.*

                    (*Inf.* IX, 61–3.)

And before a parallel passage in the *Purgatorio* about two angels and a snake we find:

Aguzza qui, lettor, ben li occhi al vero,
   chè 'l velo è ora ben tanto sottile,
   certo che 'l trapassar dentro è leggiero.†

                    (*Purg.* VIII, 19–21.)

In either case, Dante calls his reader's attention to something behind the veil of the literal sense. His words correspond so closely to the description of poet's allegory in the *Convivio* that it is difficult not to conclude that the literal sense is intentionally fictive in both, and subserves the real meaning, which is hidden. 'Il velo' is contrasted with 'il vero'. Has Dante, then, written his *Comedy* in such a way that we must look for his real meaning beneath the veil of its literal sense, which is only a beautiful lie?

We certainly would not think so if we judged his intention solely from the disputed letter which dedicates the *Paradiso* to Cangrande della Scala. Here the author (whether Dante himself or one who writes in his name) explains that the meaning of the *Comedy* is not of one kind only, and mentions the four senses familiar to any medieval expositor; but the distinctive feature of his explanation is his use of Scripture to illustrate allegory:

* 'O you who have sound minds, observe the teaching which is hidden beneath the veil of the strange lines.'

† 'Reader, focus your eyes carefully on the truth here, for the veil is now so thin that surely it is easy to penetrate it.'

The Poetry of the 'Comedy'

This method of exposition [he writes] can best be illustrated by considering how it applies to these verses: 'When Israel went out of Egypt, the house of Jacob from a people of strange language; Judah was his sanctuary, and Israel his dominion.' For if we only have regard to the letter, the meaning conveyed to us is the Exodus of the children of Israel from Egypt in the time of Moses; if we consider the allegory, we understand the meaning to be our salvation accomplished by Christ [. . .] The subject of this work, therefore, should be understood first as it is taken literally, and then according to the allegorical meaning. The subject of the whole work, then, taken only in the literal sense, is the state of souls after death, pure and simple, for on and about that turns the drift of the whole work. If the work is taken allegorically, however, the subject is Man as by his merits or demerits in exercising free will he deserves to be rewarded or punished by Justice.   (*Ep.* XIII, 7–8.)

Here, quite evidently, the *Comedy* is seen as theologian's allegory. It has a twofold subject. The literal meaning exists in its own right, just as the Exodus existed in history in its own right, and the allegory is *in facto* rather than *in verbis*, to use an Augustinian distinction.

How can we reconcile these conflicting pieces of evidence? One explanation has been proffered by the allegorist, another by the symbolist. The first would explain the *Comedy* as poet's allegory. Starting from Dante's treatment of his ode in the *Convivio*, he argues back to interpret the *Vita Nuova* in the same way also. Just as the Lady in the ode is Philosophy, so Beatrice is something else—Theology, for instance, or Grace. The literal sense of the *Vita Nuova* is then understood to be fictive, and the actual existence of a flesh-and-blood Florentine girl whom Dante loved is denied. But when he attempts to argue forward from this position to the *Comedy* his argument breaks down. Beatrice may be a 'bella menzogna' concealing a 'veritade', but what about Virgil, Statius and St Bernard? What of Hell, Purgatory and Heaven? Are these also 'belle menzogne', figments of poetic fantasy? If *they* exist in their own right, then why not Beatrice? The further the allegorist pushes his interpretation the more absurdities he is obliged to countenance, until by the rigour of logic he is forced to deny that Dante wrote the letter to Cangrande which so manifestly militates against his thesis.

Just as the allegorist is obliged to dispose of the letter, so the symbolist is bound to explain away Dante's words in the *Convivio*. His argument is this. From the letter to Cangrande we know that the literal sense of the *Comedy* exists in its own right, therefore the Beatrice of the poem existed as a historical woman who can refer to the physical body which she left on earth (*Purg.* XXXI, 47–51). But the Beatrice of the *Comedy* and of the *Vita Nuova* are one and the same, hence the *Vita Nuova* cannot be poet's allegory; therefore when Dante tells us in it that he fell in love with 'a noble lady, young and very beautiful' he means exactly what he says. But although the 'donna gentile' of the *Vita Nuova* was as real a woman as Beatrice, by the time he wrote the *Convivio* there were cogent personal reasons to compel him to declare that she was not. This old flame was proving an embarrassment to the philosopher, so he allegorized the evidence of his past passion in order to preserve his present reputation.

There can be little doubt that the symbolist's explanation

does less violence to the facts than the explanation of the allegorist, but it does not account for the admitted passages of poet's allegory in the *Comedy*, where Dante is inviting us to treat his literal sense as relatively unimportant. The solution to the problem is suggested by the example cited in the *Convivio*. For Dante, the Orpheus story is a fable; he denies historicity to the literal sense. If Ovid had sung of Samson and Delilah, the literal sense would have weighed with Dante, because he believed in the narrative of Scripture. It would no longer have been a 'veritade' concealed in a 'bella menzogna', but a 'veritade' clothed in a 'veritade'. The fall of Icarus is a beautiful lie which conceals an inner meaning, but the fall of Adam is a historical fact which conveys a moral truth. Hence Dante's distinction between poet's and theologian's allegory turns on *belief* in the literal sense of the story told—belief, in this case, not Ovid's but his own.

It was because Dante passionately believed in the Here-after which his *Comedy* describes that he likened it to the allegory of Scripture (assuming, as seems to me probable, that the letter to Cangrande is his). The literal sense of his description is not a 'bella menzogna' but a terrific reality. He was imagining something which actually existed for him—Hell, for instance, was as he pictured it, only worse. That is why we are right in interpreting his poem in the main according to the allegory of theologians. The literal sense has no more to be explained away than has the Exodus of the children of Israel, as long as the literal sense corresponds to Dante's belief about the other world. But in that literal framework he introduces elements which he

23

knows to be mythical, elements which properly belong to the 'favole de li poeti'. Such is the Gorgon's head, threatened but not seen in the ninth canto of the *Inferno*. In passages like this he is confessedly employing the allegory of poets, the allegory which Singleton calls 'this for that'.[1] But such passages are few in the *Comedy*, and the mythical creatures they introduce are distinct from the demonized agents inherited from Virgil—such as Charon and Minos —which are brought in to implement the narrative and which perform utilitarian rather than allegorical functions. Deliberate and sustained allegory as opposed to symbolism is rare in the poem, although we are introduced to it at once; for the first and clearest instance of it is the opening canto with its dark wood, right road and menacing menagerie, where most modern readers find the literal sense contrived and the poetry a little thin.

Dante's allegory or quasi-allegory (whether poet's or theologian's) is related to his poetry in the same way that 'non-musical implications' are related to programme music, in which either the music suggests the programme or the programme interprets the music. In the first case it is the art of the composer that conjures up a new dimension of meaning, just as skilful lines on a two-dimensional surface suggest depth and distance. In the second case it is the ingenuity of the interpreter that superimposes on the pattern of art a pattern of meaning which we are free to

[1] C. S. Singleton, 'Dante's Allegory', *Speculum* (January, 1950). On this subject see also Erich Auerbach, *Dante, Poet of the Secular World*, translated by Ralph Manheim (University of Chicago Press, Chicago, 1961); and Angus Fletcher, *Allegory, the Theory of a Symbolic Mode* (Cornell University Press, Ithaca, New York, 1964).

accept or reject as we please. To take two examples from Tchaikovsky: if the Festival Overture '1812' had no title, and we knew it only as opus 49, the music itself, by its thematic use of French and Russian national anthems, might suggest to us the programme in the composer's mind; but if we knew the 'Francesca da Rimini' Overture by an opus number alone, the music itself would never suggest to us the intended tragedy. The music would not cease to be music, but we would forfeit a dimension of meaning in the intention of the composer. For that dimension we need the artist as interpreter—the title, after all, is extra-musical, and belongs to the realm of interpretation.

It is always open to us to treat programme music as absolute, and it is sometimes possible for us to rule out all 'non-poetical implications' when we read the *Comedy*, but we can hardly claim in so doing that we have exhausted the author's meaning. To take an example Dante might have approved, some people believe that the middle movement of Beethoven's fourth piano concerto is intended to evoke Orpheus taming the wild animals with his lyre. Others reject the interpretation and prefer their Beethoven neat. But everyone agrees that music needs no programme to be music. It is equally true that poetry needs no allegory to be poetry, and no amount of allegorization can add poetic value to a poem. What Dante meant to convey to us by the figure of Matelda in the Terrestrial Paradise (to cite an unsolved riddle) is still discussed by commentators, and rightly so, for such discussion falls within their province; but to appraise the poet's art we need not look beyond the literal sense, in which with telling effect he has created the figure of

> una donna soletta che si gia
>> cantando e scegliendo fior da fiore
>> ond'era pinta tutta la sua via.*
>
> (*Purg.* XXVIII, 40–2.)

Here the music suggests no programme, the poetry no allegory. Instead the words wake echoes of the Sweet New Style and herald Petrarch and Politian—and we are well content. If we seek interpretation, we must find it elsewhere, and superimpose it on the poetry: but at best it will be an optional extra. Yet, if we were assured with all possible assurance that Beethoven intended to evoke Orpheus, or that Dante intended Matelda to symbolize the Active Life, would not this fact open for us a new dimension of meaning?

The question prompts a vital distinction as far as Dante the poet is concerned, for meaning of this sort is suggested either by the artist *qua* artist, or the artist *qua* interpreter, or by an interpreter other than the artist. In the latter two cases there is no contradiction involved in evaluating the work of art without reference to the interpretation. Great artists are sometimes misleading interpreters of their best work; when an embarrassed Tasso, for instance, tells us that his *Gerusalemme Liberata* is all a moral allegory we are unconvinced. We have been spared the exhaustive commentary which Dante would have written on his *Comedy* if he had lived, for it would have been as prosaic as the

* 'A solitary lady who went along singing and picking flower after flower with which all her path was decked.'

poem is poetic; but Dante the interpreter already exists cheek by jowl with Dante the poet, and within the *Comedy* too. For example, it is Dante the poet who creates Geryon, that biblico-classical monster of impeccable pedigree, but it is Dante the interpreter who labels him 'quella sozza imagine di froda'* (*Inf.* xvii, 7). We may delight in the *imagine* but repudiate the label, believing (with some modern critics) that Geryon is not Fraud but Geryon, and that his function in the poem is not to deceive, but to bear two poets on his back as he descends through the air in wheeling flight. It is only when the artist *qua* artist suggests the dimension of meaning which is allegory that we are carried by the compulsion of his art.

Such is Dante's poetic genius that time and again he compels us to explore his meaning—and how vast the dimension of that meaning is! Here is an encyclopaedic affirmation of faith, a poet's *Summa* which is immeasurably more than rhymed Aquinas. Indeed it might be maintained that the greatness of the *Comedy* begins with its subject, if the stature of a poem is enhanced by the magnitude of its matter, for even today no greater theme can be conceived than this universal vision of human destiny which tempted one nineteenth-century pope to speak of a 'fifth gospel' (inaccurately, of course, since the place of Christ in Dante's Heaven is largely usurped by Beatrice). Some would-be great poems are limited by the triviality of their subject-matter; but even an indifferent poet treating a great theme can sometimes achieve memorable effects by evoking, however clumsily, the shadow of a greatness

* 'That filthy image of Fraud.'

independent of his wit. A poem must be bad indeed (as bad as Trissino's *L'Italia Liberata dai Goti*) if nothing of the splendour of its subject rubs off upon its images.

Dante's subject is neither circumscribed nor trivial: in his *Comedy* the sky is the limit and the goal is God. It is the widest of cosmic canvases, this vision of the other world in which our world is mirrored. Every great motive is there: faith, hope and charity; passion, patriotism and pageantry; sin, salvation and sanctity; guilt, grace and glory—the whole human predicament, the entire divine remedy. It even boasts its ration of science-fiction and space-travel. But the presence of all these ingredients does not insure a work of art, any more than eggs, butter and herbs guarantee an omelette. Without poetic genius Dante might have made a hash of the finest raw materials, which he did not create but found ready to his hand.

For he was not responsible for his theme in the same way that Ariosto was responsible for the subject-matter of his *Orlando Furioso*. Dante no more invented the Hereafter than Cimabue invented the Madonna and Child. His culture was intricately compounded of Christian and classical elements, and the fabric of his *Comedy* is woven from the warp of pagan antiquity and the weft of Christianity. When we say that he was a profoundly *original* poet we obviously do not mean that he originated Hell, Purgatory and Heaven, or even the idea of a living man visiting the other world and describing what he saw there. He found his theme in the conscience of Christendom. Any other poet might have handled it, because it existed independently of every poet. Nor was Dante responsible for the greatness of his theme, which remained great even in the hands of a minor poet like Matteo Palmieri.

The *Comedy*, then, is not a creation of pure fantasy, like *The Rime of the Ancient Mariner*, in which theme and treatment cohere in unique synthesis. Dante's Virgil is an evocation of someone who exists apart from his imagination, and so are his Lucifer and his God. The same thing can be said of the central narrative thread that runs through the poem. The poet's pilgrimage is indeed a mystery tour, but not in the popular sense of an outing-with-destination-unknown. We know the end from the beginning—the very title gives the clue. Dante's travels are not intended to be fantastic, like Baron von Münch-hausen's: they are intended to be credible. Hence the *Comedy* is not pure fiction in which anything might happen: it is controlled by a reality independent of itself. Dante is describing the Universe which is.

That Universe is not a 'fortuitous concourse of atoms', nor has it a structure incomprehensible to the human mind. It boasts an architectonic cohesion and unity which reflect the mind of God. Through creation, revelation and experience its structure may be apprehended by the finite intellect and in turn reflected in a work of art. Nothing less than this has Dante attempted in his poem. He has created a structure in words to illustrate the structure which God has created in fact—not only the physical structure of celestial and terrestrial bodies, but also the interacting rational structure of the mind and moral structure of the heart. The Universe which we explore in the *Comedy* has a majesty that compels our admiration, but it raises two fundamental questions which have taxed the minds of the most influential school of Italian critics in our day. Is Dante's structure the work of the intellect or the imagination? Does the structure of his poetry entail the poetry of his structure?

Natalino Sapegno has already pronounced a weighty and authoritative verdict on the critical distinction between 'structure' and 'poetry' in the *Comedy*, and I have no wish either to poach on his preserves (which would be impertinent) or add to his judgement (which would be impossible). Nevertheless, it would be difficult to discuss the poetry of the *Comedy* today without hinting at this central critical issue, which I shall approach from a different angle. For no one can scratch the surface of twentieth-century Dante criticism without discovering the name of Benedetto Croce, the most eminent humanist that the New Italy has produced. It was in the theory of aesthetics that he first gained a world reputation two generations ago with the publication of his *Estetica* in 1902. He defined art in general as 'intuition' and poetry in particular as 'lyric intuition', and declared (quite rightly) that it is easier to say what poetry is *not* than what it is. For instance, it is not history, theology, philosophy or morals, because all these disciplines deal in concepts, whereas poetry is not conceptual but intuitive. In so far as any significant combination of sounds expresses a concept, to that extent it falls outside the definition of poetry because it is the product of the practical rather than the intuitive function of the mind. Therefore, however cogent the conceptual element in a poem may be it can add nothing to its poetry: as poetry it stands or falls by the element of lyric intuition within it. What lies outside this definition is non-poetry, and it is the primary task of the literary critic to distinguish the poetry from the non-poetry in a poem.

It was inevitable that sooner or later Croce should apply his aesthetic formula to the greatest of all Italian poems. This he did with devastating effect in a slim volume entitled *La Poesia di Dante* which was intended to mark the last commemoration of the poet, in 1921, the sixth centenary of his death.[1] Some people said that it marked the occasion all too effectively by killing the poet stone-dead. Croce himself maintained that the truth was just the reverse—that he had in fact brought the authentic poet to life. Whoever was right, no subsequent critic of Dante can ignore his thesis, which is that most Dantists (some of whom he calls 'Dantomaniacs') confound things which differ. They like the *Comedy* and think its author a great poet in virtue not of the poetry in it but the non-poetry: the alluring allegory, towering theological architecture, Christian philosophy, scintillating ratiocination, lofty morality, and so on. Now all these things, says Croce, add nothing to the poetry of the poem, which still stands or falls by the lyric intuition that informs it. Being himself an agnostic subjective idealist, he discounts the very elements in the *Comedy* which have induced Christian posterity to call it 'Divine'. The allegory is part of the *allotria* which is non-poetry, and does not interest him; not

[1] English version by Douglas Ainslie, *The Poetry of Dante* (London, 1922).

31

only the long pageant which Dante shows us in the Terrestrial Paradise but also the *Comedy* itself is reduced to the dimensions of a pantomime, as though a man should go to Mass and see nothing but the posturing of a priest. It is not, of course, that the poem is judged to be unpoetical by Croce, who would hardly have been the consummate critic he was without a developed appreciation of Dante's art; but the poetry is only to be found in patches of lyric intuition which glimmer like oases in the conceptual desert. Such patches, for instance, as the episode of Paolo and Francesca in the fifth, Farinata in the tenth, Brunetto Latini in the fifteenth, Ulysses in the twenty-sixth, and Ugolino in the thirty-third cantos of the *Inferno*, to limit ourselves to the first of the three canticles. It is on such moments of intuition (which are varied, rich and many) that the poetry of the *Comedy* must be appraised.

The most controversial chapter in Croce's book deals with the structure of the *Comedy* in relation to its poetry. Its basic contention is that although the Hereafter with its three realms of Hell, Purgatory and Heaven is the ostensible theme of the poem, it is not really the 'dominant poetic motive of the poetry' at all. There is too little Hell in Dante's *Inferno*, too little Heaven in his *Paradiso*, and too much of *this* world in the next. The other world of damnation, purgation and bliss has not been poetically evoked because it has not been poetically felt. Like any other narrator, Dante has been at pains to construct an imaginative arena for his action with the maximum possible verisimilitude, and being endowed with a formidable intellect he has succeeded admirably. But the resulting structure is the product of the practical activity of the mind rather than of that formulative function which Croce calls intuition: hence by definition the practical structure is excluded from the poetry. At one point Croce specifically contrasts the *Comedy* with Shakespeare's major plays, in which (he says) the structure springs from the poetic motive, and there is not structure and poetry, but all is homogeneous, all is poetry. Dante's description of the 'triplice regno' is not properly poetry, and it cannot be called science. What is it, then? According to Croce, it is a 'theological novel' that provides the continuum for the patches of lyric intuition, which appear like rambler roses adorning a massive but utilitarian building.

The influence of Croce's aesthetic was paramount in Italy between the Wars, and moulded a generation of critics. It became the fashion to write commentaries on the *Comedy* which labelled one passage 'structure' and another 'poetry', just as dutiful divinity students marked their Pentateuchs with J, E, D and P. We may illustrate this cold-blooded anatomy by quoting two tercets from the best-known canto of the whole *Comedy*. Here are the opening lines:

> Così discesi del cerchio primaio
> giù nel secondo, che men luogo cinghia,
> e tanto più dolor, che punge a guaio.*
>
> (*Inf.* v, 1–3.)

That is structure, and belongs to the theological novel. The hero proceeds from point *A* to point *B*, a practical and

---

* 'So I descended from the first circle down into the second, which encloses less space, and so much more pain that it stings to lamentation.'

necessary step if we are to get on with the narrative; but the novelist does not evoke the movement, he merely goes through the motions. And here is a moment of climax later in the canto:

> Amor, ch'al cor gentil ratto s'apprende,
>   prese costui de la bella persona
>   che mi fu tolta; e 'l modo ancor m'offende.★
>
> (*Inf.* v, 100–2.)

That is poetry, the flash of lyric intuition, the authentic notation of the heart. Francesca is moved, Dante is moved, the reader is moved—unless he is irreverent enough to detect the stilnovistic rhetoric.

We may readily agree that there is a marked difference of tone between these two tercets, but here is a third to complicate the issue:

> Luogo è in inferno detto Malebolge,
>   tutto di pietra di color ferrigno,
>   come la cerchia che dintorno il volge.†
>
> (*Inf.* xviii, 1–3.)

Is this structure, or poetry? Structure without doubt, for it is a piece of Hell's topography and a necessary background to the action of the theological novel; but just as evidently it is a moment of poetry, or lyric intuition, in which with striking economy of means Dante has transported us to a

---

★ 'Love, which is quickly kindled in the noble heart, seized this man for the beautiful body which was taken from me; and the way [he loved me] overpowers me still (or, and the manner [of my death] still afflicts me).'

† 'There is a place in Hell called Malebolge, all of iron-coloured stone, like the circle which girds it round.'

known place of dread and despair. Hell he has inherited from Virgil and the Bible, but he has conjured Malebolge from his imagination at the beck of genius; for these lines are both the description of an excogitated structure and the poetic evocation of a felt environment. Here concept and image fuse, and the distinction between poetry and non-poetry is annulled.

It seems, then, that there are times when the structure of Dante's poetry admits the poetry of his structure. Indeed, some of the most stupendous of his effects are structural. Purgatory was created by the Catholic Church, but Dante created its mountain setting, and it is one of his most original creations: what is Mount Purgatory but a poetic image? We do not see it, as Ulysses saw it, 'bruna per la distanza', looming upon the horizon of the Southern Hemisphere

> alta tanto
> quanto veduta non avea alcuna.*
>
> (*Inf.* XXVI, 133–5.)

Dante does not present it to *us* in that way, but suggests its calculated perspective and dimensions little by little as the second canticle unfolds. He does not flash his full-formed image on our inward eye, but reveals it glimpse by glimpse until we see it steadily and see it whole. It is misleading here to speak of a moment of lyric intuition; we begin to read the first canto of the *Purgatorio* with no visual impression of its setting, but find that when we stand with Dante in the Terrestrial Paradise at the end of canto thirty-three we are fully in his picture.

* 'Dim with distance...so high that I had seen none of such height.'

Yet even if we read the second canticle from end to end we may miss the prime effect which the creator of Mount Purgatory has intended, and that is the effect of contrast. We must experience Hell before we can appreciate Purgatory. We must be fearfully confined in the starless foetor of the Pit before we can enjoy the sky-space of the sea-dawn and all the vernal beauty of the sunlit slopes. The contrast between the descent of Hell and the ascent of Purgatory is not only a moral truth propounded by the allegory, but also an impressive poetic effect which springs from the structure of the poem.

What, then, of the distinction between poetry and structure? Upon examination we find that the theatre which Dante has constructed for his drama is often as much a work of the imagination as the play itself, and works of the imagination admit of no distinction of kind. There is no 'poetry of things', declares Croce, only the 'poetry of poetry'. We may agree with him, and judge that when Byron hailed the prospect of a free Italy as the 'poetry of politics' he spoke with poetic licence. Words are the poet's only medium, and if by this means Dante has created in us his visual image of the structure of the Hereafter, we have no need to postulate the poetry of things, for what we experience is the poetry of poetry. Croce's conclusions may follow from the premises of his aesthetic, but those premises are drawn from an inadequate psychology which ignores the function of the mind in co-ordinating images and fashioning a master-image. The result is a virtual negation of the possibility of epic or narrative (as distinct from lyric) poetry. If we ask how Homer evokes the total image of the Trojan war, and Virgil suggests the majesty of the Roman Empire, or how Camoëns, Milton and Goethe create in us the pattern of their themes transcending the sum of their lyric moments, the answer must surely be that it is by the same art with which Dante communicates to us his master-image of the ordered structure of the Universe of God.

'Lyric intuition' may tell us much, but it does not tell us all. Poetry, like electricity, is known by its effects: its essential quiddity escapes us. Electricity is not light, nor heat, nor shock—all these are non-electricity; yet we know when we touch a live wire that electricity exists. Poetry is not style, nor technique, nor even feeling—all these are non-poetry; yet we know, when we hear the quickening word, that poetry exists. We hunt it, as boys chase butterflies, with the net of definition; but the net is full of holes, and poetry eludes us. 'Emotion recollected in tranquillity,' sighs Wordsworth—'A scratching of the back,' shrugs Housman. But poetry is not emotion, nor is it pastime: it is both these things *plus* poetry. The ineffable is not made effable by labels: the word 'intuition' tells us no more than the word 'electricity'.

But if the spring and source of poetry in the poet is unsearchable and the creative act defies his own analysis, for the poet's audience the effects of poetry begin in the ear. Even an unlettered jockey might dig the sound and rhythm of Virgil's

quadripedante putrem sonitu quatit ungula campum,[1]

and on this rudimentary level of onomatopoeia the

[1] *Aeneid*, VIII, 596.

37

Comedy has as much to offer as the *Aeneid*. Dante's interest in the musicality of verse is patent from his prose writings on poetic technique, and with so superb a craftsman we can be sure that the vocalic melody of his poem which ravishes our senses is not accidental; for he displays not only a near-perfect control of *terza rima* (not the easiest of forms to handle) but also a mastery of words which by their very disposition in the poetic period captivate the ear. We must beware the danger of overstressing the appeal of sound without meaning, for it is easy enough to parody vocalic melody; nevertheless many of Dante's admirers have savoured the aural impact of some of his verses before they fully understood their meaning, for the *Comedy* possesses to a high degree that haunting, echoing quality which is one of the hall-marks of poetry. When snatches like

> la concreata e perpetua sete
> del deiforme regno*   (*Par.* ii, 19–20.)

invade our consciousness, even if their full significance is unexplored (and Dante has more to offer us than we can assimilate), we know that what we hear has the authentic ring of great poetry. But if we have more than an inkling of the poet's meaning, we shall find that sound and sense often complement one another to a marvel. Listen, for instance, to this passage which likens the wailing of damned souls, buffeted by the never-resting hurricane of Hell, to the moaning of the storm-tossed sea:

> Ora incomincian le dolenti note
> a farmisi sentire; or son venuto
> là dove molto pianto mi percuote.

* 'The inborn and unceasing thirst for the Godlike realm....'

38

The Poetry of the 'Comedy'

Io venni in luogo d'ogni luce muto,
  che mugghia come fa mar per tempesta,
  se da contrari venti è combattuto.★

(Inf. v, 25–30.)

It is because we sense that the sound of Dante's verse heralds, yet shrouds, a world of meaning that his music echoes in our ears and haunts our minds. Nothing cloys more surely than mere melody, and if this were all that he afforded us he would have languished in limbo with Swinburne long since. It is the infinite suggestion of what lies beyond that lures us forward, as he himself was impelled beyond Hell-gate to apprehend the ultimate meaning of the Universe.

But however great the appeal of his poetry to the ear may be, it is less essential to Dante than to almost any other poet. He is not dependent on his music for the communication of his mind, and that is why he triumphs even in translation. Immeasurably greater is his appeal to the eye, or more exactly, to the visual imagination. The *Comedy* opens with an image and closes with an image, and from end to end it enchants the eye like some encyclopaedic picture-book. Indeed, for visual imagery Dante has no equal. There are, I think, two reasons for this. The first is that he saw so clearly and penetratingly himself; when he turned his *occhi grifagni* on the world of Man and Nature he saw far more than lesser men see. Epistemologists describe the

★ 'Now the doleful strains begin to reach my ear; now I have come to a place where much lamentation assails me. I entered a region devoid of all light, which bellows like the sea in storm when it is fought by opposing winds.'

co-ordinating function of the mind in perception, and Dante's is a master mind: the whole sculptured image of this world in the *Comedy* proclaims the activity of his *mens creatrix*. And what is true of his natural vision of this world is true also of his imagination of the world to come: it is clear, it is in perfect focus, it is concrete, and it carries conviction. We see what we have a mind to see. The clear mind sees more clearly because it knows what it is looking for, and the ordered mind sees order. Most readers of his poem would agree that the mind of Dante is a spectroscope of unexampled clarity and order.

The second reason for the vivid appeal of his visual imagery is that his art has the same definition as his sight. The image he sees in focus he projects in focus, often with the hard brilliance of diamond upon glass. Like the great Florentine painters of his own and succeeding generations, Dante has a developed feeling for significant form, and a practised hand at so tracing lyric outline that it suggests the sculpturesque. This suggestion of the sculpturesque is, I believe, the essence of his pictorial art, which in turn lends itself to illustration. I have no wish to overstate my case, or speak of Dante only in superlatives. There are peaks and troughs in the *Comedy*, just as there are in any long poem. Here we stumble on the primitive rigidity of the Byzantine, and there the grotesquery of a Bosch; but at his brilliant best the artist in him is Giotto, Raphael and Michelangelo in one.

Perhaps Dante's appeal to the visual imagination is first felt and most easily studied in his similes, those incomparable gems which gleam from almost every page of the

Comedy and which display the range of his experience and observation. Often they are drawn from domestic life, and picture the kitchen, the stable, and the world below the salt. Just as often they recall the family with its affections and relationships from which the poet was an exile. More frequently still they enshrine vignettes from the life of artisans and labourers, or reveal imperishable glimpses of Nature. A few deft touches, and the stage is set; an eyeful of sharp-etched images, and the time, place, sound and sensation are evoked:

> E come a gracidar si sta la rana
>   col muso fuor dell'acqua, quando sogna
>   di spigolar sovente la villana;
> livide, insin là dove appar vergogna
>   eran l'ombre dolenti ne la ghiaccia,
>   mettendo i denti in nota di cicogna.★
>
> (Inf. XXXII, 31–36.)

Whether Dante's source is Ovid or the duck-pond hardly affects the impact of his art, for in the *Comedy*—as in all great poems—life reflects literature and literature mirrors life. How typical, how telling, and how true are his thumb-nail sketches of ordinary men, caught in an attitude and immortalized in an instant! When the lustful behold in Dante a man alive in Purgatory

> Non altrimenti stupido si turba
>   lo montanaro, e rimirando ammuta,
>   quando rozzo e salvatico s'inurba,

★ 'And as the frog, in order to croak, sits with its muzzle out of the water, when the peasant woman often dreams of gleaning, so livid in the ice up to the point where shame appears were the suffering shades, setting their teeth to the stork's note.'

che ciascun'ombra fece in sua paruta.★
(*Purg.* XXVI, 67–70.)

But profound though his understanding of men is, Dante draws his most moving similes from bird-life, and at times they are breathtaking in their tenderness and comprehension. Never was the lark more poignantly portrayed than in this limpid tercet:

> Quale allodetta che 'n aere si spazia
> prima cantando, e poi tace contenta
> de l'ultima dolcezza che la sazia...†
> (*Par.* XX, 73–5.)

But there's the rub: the tercet which follows and completes the comparison is far from limpid—in fact it is dense with theological implications:

> tal mi sembiò l'imago de la 'mprenta
> de l'etterno piacere, al cui disio
> ciascuna cosa qual ella è diventa.‡
> (*Par.* XX, 76–8.)

For the *Comedy* is not merely a kaleidoscope of image succeeding image, a pageant of sound and sight. Just as the appeal to the ear is transcended by the appeal to the eye, so the appeal to the eye is transcended by the appeal to the

---

★ 'Each shade adopted an expression just like that of the country cousin who becomes dazed with wonder and gazes about him open-mouthed when, rough and uncouth, he comes to town.'

† 'Like the lark that soars in the air, singing at first, and then is silent, content with the last sweetness which fully satisfies her...'

‡ '...so seemed to me the image of the imprint of the eternal pleasure, by desiring which each thing becomes what it really is.'

mind. The soaring lark transports us into a dimension of meaning in which Man's questing nature finds its fulfilment in the justice of God. This is the constant purpose of Dante's imagery. All his similes depict the unseen from the seen, the unknown from the known, using the fixed point of reference in our familiar world to project us into the unfamiliar realm of his imagining. But inevitably, because his visual image is so evocative and his analogy so apt, some of the unfamiliarity of that realm is lost by the comparison. At the touch of poetic genius the dead come alive, sit up and talk—and what should they talk about but the world they shared in common with the poet? So back we come from Hell to Francesca's bedroom, to the Casentino, to the famine-tower at Pisa. The eternal infinity beyond death is timed and spaced. Of course we cannot have it both ways at once: the more real and solid we feel the other world to be, the more like our own it is, and the less we sense its otherness. And the less conscious we become of its otherness, the less we experience its terror—its ecstasy—its mystery. Familiarity begins to breed the first suspicion of contempt. That is why some critics have grumbled at the 'homeliness' of Dante's Hereafter. Heaven indeed should be our home-from-home, for God has set eternity in our hearts, but ought we to feel at home in Purgatory and Hell?

That we do so in any measure is due to the poetic effect of Dante's analogy, appealing to the mind from this world to the next. Those fixed points of reference in the Here-and-Now from which he projects his Hereafter are not only the familiar frogs and larks and peasants of his similes, but

43

embrace the institutions, principles and personalities of the City of Man, set between the City of God and the City of Dis. Indeed the first and firmest point of all is his native Florence. Shakespeare is sometimes called the 'Bard of Stratford-on-Avon', but that is just what he was not: we may search his works from cover to cover and find no patriot's praise, no zealous rebuke, for his native town. But Dante with his love-hate complex cannot leave Florence alone. Florence makes him, Florence breaks him, but to the end of his life he remains incurably, passionately, vindictively Florentine. Surely there never was any poet so universal yet local in his outlook, and it is just this sense of locality in universality, of universality in locality, which lends enchantment to his poem. It becomes not only the microcosm of one medieval Catholic Florentine, but also the vision of the whole human race at any time and in any place in so far as the poet in Man transcends the particular in the universal, yet portrays the universal in the particular. For the 'sacred poem to which both Heaven and Earth have set their hand' (*Par.* xxv, 1–2) is prefaced by those pungent words: 'Here begins the Comedy of Dante Alighieri, a Florentine by birth but not by behaviour,'[1] and even when he is in the depths of Hell or the heights of Heaven the visionary never loses sight of Florence as his fixed point of reference on earth, from which—meta-phorically—he measures the mileage to the City of Dis and the City of God. If the barbarians coming from the far North, on seeing Rome and her mighty works, were amazed,

[1] Incipit Comedia Dantis Alagherii Florentini natione, non moribus.

io, che al divino da l'umano,
  a l'etterno dal tempo era venuto,
  e di Fiorenza in popol giusto e sano,
di che stupor dovea esser compiuto!*

               (*Par.* XXXI, 37–40.)

It is the passage from the human to the divine, from time to the eternal, from the particular to the universal, from the City of Man to the City of God that Dante proposes as the supreme end of his poetry. Like Abraham when God called him from his native Ur, so Dante when he was banished from his native Florence 'looked for a city which hath foundations, whose builder and maker is God'.[1] His search and his discovery culminate in the *Comedy*'s third canticle, which is not only better than anything else he wrote, but probably better than any other poetry ever written. Here, pre-eminently, the greatness of the poem is seen in the attempt as well as in the achievement, for the task which the poet has set himself in the *Paradiso* is almost superhuman. The *Inferno* and the *Purgatorio* are imagined on the human level, with the poetic focus on Man; but this third canticle is always striving to transcend human nature and reach up to God. At its outset Dante confesses

       Trasumanar significar per verba
         non si poria—†   (*Par.* I, 70–1.)

yet that is just what he is attempting to do in the *Paradiso*: to express the inexpressible in words.

---

[1] Hebrews xi. 10 (A.V.).

* 'With what stupor must not *I* have been filled, who had come to the divine from the human, to the eternal from time, and from Florence to a people just and sane!'

† 'To pass beyond human nature cannot be expressed in words.'

On the highest Authority we know that men love darkness rather than light, because their deeds are evil, and it is far easier to make a convincing picture of vice than of virtue. The degrees and modes of blessedness and joy are immeasurably harder to depict and differentiate than the degrees and modes of purification and punishment. Hell is a palpable pit with granite bastions, Purgatory a solid mountain firm underfoot, but Heaven is all up in the air with no familiar landscape to inspire the poet. It is the ultimate triumph of Dante's art that he has carried us with him from planet to planet, has made sanctity attractive to the soul and Heaven intelligible to the mind.

From our reading of the *Paradiso* we take away no such gallery of human portraits as from the earlier canticles. The focus is less and less on Man, and increasingly on God. Even if we remember Cacciaguida, it is because we picture him back in Florence 'dentro da la cerchia antica'* (*Par.* xv, 97)—as sculpturesque an image as we may find in Hell. What takes the place of the excogitated structure is not so much the Dionysian disposition of the heavenly bodies as the cardinal doctrines of the Christian faith, which are seen to be the foundations of the Celestial City and the pillars that uphold the Universe—the justice and the love of God. And it is here supremely, inimitably, unforgettably that Dante displays the sovereign quality of genius by creating in us anew (and it is the final proof of poetry) that thirst for the beauty of holiness and hunger after God which grows with the growing light until we see His Face.

* 'Within the ancient circle of her walls.'

3

RELIGION AND PHILOSOPHY
IN DANTE

KENELM FOSTER, O.P.

We commonly think of Dante as both a religious and a philosophical poet; and, so doing, we commonly assume that there is a difference of some kind between poetry on the one hand and religion and philosophy on the other; we imply that to be a poet is not the same as to be religious or philosophical. This distinction is supported by ordinary experience and I need not labour it here. But the phrase 'a religious and philosophical poet' also implies some difference between religion and philosophy; otherwise, why two epithets rather than one? And this point must detain me a little before proceeding to the task assigned me by the title of my paper; for clearly I cannot assume, at this stage, that the relation between religion and philosophy in Dante's work is either an identity or a non-identity, or, if a non-identity, either a harmony or tension; my task being to show just which relation is best supported by evidence. And we need, to start with, some working definition of the two terms whose relationship is in question.

In ordinary usage the terms religion and philosophy are somewhat vague; moreover, they overlap; what in one context we call a man's religion, in another we may speak of as his philosophy, and vice versa. Still, even as commonly used, each term has a meaning or a set of meanings proper to itself. By religion is commonly meant a belief in, and corresponding attitude towards, some power that controls the universe and is entitled to worship and obedience; whereas by philosophy we usually mean a certain kind of knowledge, or the pursuit of it, understood as having to do with general causes and principles. And, as regards religion, we can, I think, take a further step, still on the basis of common usage—a step that incidentally will bring into view, though still remotely, an important aspect of the situation which Dante had to face as he grew to intellectual maturity. For if we assume a distinction between belief and understanding—between *fides* and *scientia* or *intellectus*, as Dante's scholastic masters would have said—we can surely go on to say that the element of belief is less distinctive of religion than the element of worship and obedience; for belief might turn into understanding, and yet, if worship and obedience continued, religion itself would continue. In other words, religion is more a moral commitment than it is any given condition of the mind as cognitive, that is, as intellect: whether that condition be mere belief or clear knowledge is incidental to religion as such, which is essentially a moral quality in the will. Philosophy, on the other hand, is essentially intellectual; it is a desire for, or possession of, understanding; and if it connotes an act of the will—apart from the mere will to understand—this is incidental to its nature as philosophy. The philosopher as such is fulfilled in simply knowing; the religious man in worshipping and obeying.

The relevance of these considerations will, I hope, appear

in due course; but three rather general observations arising from them may be useful at this point. (*a*) In the tradition which formed Dante's mind philosophy (understood, more or less, as defined above) was of course regarded as distinct from religion, and was even allowed in practice a certain limited independence of theology, the systematization of religious belief. Yet philosophy then had a close connexion with religion (since the eighteenth century largely lost), in that nearly all philosophers thought of themselves as engaged, like the theologians though from a different point of view, in the study of God: they identified the ultimate cause or principle, which they sought to discover by reason, with the God of their religious tradition.[1] (*b*) But the difference in point of view naturally led to tensions and friction in practice, and these in turn to various 'solutions'. The solution of Averroes, for example, in the twelfth century (worked out, of course, in relation to the authority of the Koran, not of the Bible) was simply and in principle to subordinate religion to philosophy; but this no Western thirteenth century thinker, however imbued with Averroism, ventured openly to do. A contrary solution, that of making philosophy ancillary to theology, was worked out, in various ways, and from different philosophical positions, by Christian theologians like

[1] Thus the late thirteenth-century Averroist Boethius of Dacia defines the *summum bonum*, in the contemplation of which the philosopher finds all the felicity possible to man in this life, as 'ens primum secundum philosophos, et secundum sanctos Deus benedictus' (see M. Grabmann, 'Die *Opuscula de Summo Bono sive De vita philosophi* und *De sompniis* des Boetius von Dacien', *Archives d'histoire doctrinale et littéraire du moyen âge*, VI, 1932, 287–317; and *Mittelalterliches Geistesleben*, Munich, 1936–1956, II, pp. 200–24).

Aquinas and Bonaventure. And then there was the compromise associated with the so-called 'Latin Averroists', the most famous of whom was Siger of Brabant, whom Dante thought worthy of a place in the *Paradiso* (x, 133-8): let the philosopher follow reason freely as far as it may lead him, even to the point of speculative unorthodoxy, provided only that he be prepared to admit *in practice* that from the theologian's point of view—not, certainly, his own— his rational conclusions might be false.[1] (c) In the doctrinal writings of the time this tension and these solutions usually appear in the context of disputes about the speculative competence of philosophy: was a given point of doctrine demonstrable, or was it purely a matter of faith? What was generally at issue—directly or indirectly—was the boundary-limit of rational speculation, the reach of its competence to determine what is or is not *true*. Much less conspicuous (though not absent) was the practical question, whether philosophy can be taken as a guide to life; and if so, how far: in concrete terms, whether and how far the kind of practical humane wisdom sketched out by Aristotle in the Nicomachean Ethics could be accepted by Christians. But it is chiefly to this last area of discussion, to this moral and practical issue, that we are led, I think, if we search the works of Dante for signs of the tension I am speaking of. It appears in him mainly, I think, as the effect on a Christian mind of a very strong and very personal

[1] For useful introductions to the matters touched on in this paragraph, see: E. Gilson, *History of Christian Philosophy in the Middle Ages* (London, 1955), pp. 235-427; M. D. Chenu, *Introduction à l'étude de S. Thomas d'Aquin* (Paris, 1950); F. Van Steenberghen, *The Philosophical Movement in the Thirteenth Century* (London, 1955).

attraction to Aristotelian ethics. This is the general thesis that I shall try to maintain in what follows.

And this is to say in advance that in treating of Dante's ideas I shall be selective, confining myself for the most part to one fundamental topic; and with regard even to this topic I shall not be greatly concerned with questions of influence and derivation. The task of relating, in detail, Dante's ideas to their time-context and background is one which very few men alive today are qualified to attempt, and I am not of their number.[1] I know enough of this most intricate subject to be sure that I could not handle it with confidence, at any rate as regards the details; for there are certain generalities about Dante's relation to traditions and influences that I can maintain with some assurance, and some of these it will be as well to state forthwith: they will serve to introduce certain features of the poet's outlook and mentality that seem to me especially significant from the point of view I have chosen to adopt.

First, then, I am sure that Dante's works provide no evidence that he ever renounced Catholic Christianity, of his ever becoming either an unbeliever or a heretic; and

[1] The chief authority on Dante's thought in relation to its historical background is Bruno Nardi, a full bibliography of whose work, down to 1955, is in *Medioevo e Rinascimento: Studi in onore di B. Nardi*, 2 vol. (Florence, 1956) (pp. 907–27). Nardi's most important works in this field since 1955 are: *Studi di filosofia medievale* (Rome, 1960), and *Dal 'Convivio' alla 'Commedia' (Sei saggi danteschi)* (Rome, 1960). See also E. Gilson, *Dante et la philosophie* (Paris, 1939; reprinted 1954); G. Busnelli's commentary in the 'Edizione Nazionale' of Dante's *Convivio*, 2 vol. (Florence, 1934 and 1937); J. A. Mazzeo, *Structure and Thought in the 'Paradiso'*, and *Medieval Cultural Tradition in Dante's 'Comedy'* (Cornell University Press, 1958 and 1960 respectively); M. Grabmann, *Mittelalterliches Geistesleben*, 3 vol. (Munich, 1936–56), espec. I, 332 ff., III, 197–212.

this is not something one can simply take for granted in a man of his time and milieu. On the other hand I am equally sure that faith and reason in him did not go easily hand in hand. He had enormous intellectual energy and he belonged to a world that was in its own way intellectually highly sophisticated. The second half of the thirteenth century, when Dante grew to manhood, saw the general acceptance as the chief sources of philosophical and scientific culture for every educated European, whether cleric or layman, of the works of Aristotle and of his Greek and Arabic commentators. But the cost of that acceptance was a profound disturbance of the Christian mind, an intellectual *crise de croissance* as great as any in Christian history, and in its effects probably greater than any down to our own time. If you would form some idea of this crisis and of the dialectical strenuousness that it called for on the orthodox side, read Aquinas where he is at grips with the Averroistic theses on the rational soul and its relation to the body (*Summa theol.* 1 a. lxxvi, lxxix; *Contra Gentiles*, 11, 59–78); or, for a wider—and more sensational—view, read the 219 theses condemned by the bishop of Paris, Etienne Tempier, in 1277 (when Dante was nearly twelve), theses that were circulating in the Arts Faculty of the University, and of which Gilson observes: 'On croirait entendre, non pas même Fontenelle, toujours si prudent en ses propos, mais Voltaire lorsqu'il est sûr de l'impunité.' For example: 'that the Christian religion is an obstacle to progress in knowledge'; 'that there are fables and falsehoods in Christianity as in other religions'; 'that what the theologians say is all based on fables'; 'that there is no life more

noble than to devote oneself to (secular) philosophy';
'that happiness is to be had in this life and not in another'.
This last proposition is particularly relevant, I think, to the
way Dante personally felt the tension between faith and
reason.[1]

But he felt it also, of course, with regard to more strictly
speculative matters. It is clear that, with other Western
intellectuals of his time, Dante found rational difficulties in,
for example, the doctrine of creation *ex nihilo*; in the
relation of matter to spirit, both in the cosmos generally
and in human nature; in the nature and range of free will.
In the *Comedy* he faces each of these basic problems and
resolves them in an orthodox sense, but certainly without
recourse to mere authority. For him (at any rate when he
came to write the *Comedy*) these were matters which
reason—at least as guided by faith—was competent to in-
vestigate and decide; and Dante had clearly not shirked the
dialectic they involved before he came to weave his conclusions into the close-knit texture of *Purgatorio* and
Paradiso. Another, more specifically 'Christian', problem
gave him more trouble, that of the salvation of the un-
baptized. Here, since no purely rational solution was
available, the only course for a believing Christian was to
submit his intellect to the mystery of God's judgement;
and Dante duly makes his submission on this point in the

[1] For the text of Tempier's condemnation see: *Chartularium Uni-
versitatis Parisiensis*, ed. Denifle and Chatelain, 4 vol. (Paris, 1889–97)
(vol. I, no. 4); also the classic work of P. Mandonnet, *Siger de Brabant et
l'avérroïsme latin au XIII siècle*, 2 vol. (Louvain, 1908–11) (II, 175–91).
The words quoted from Gilson are taken from *La philosophie au moyen
âge* (Paris, 1944), p. 559.

great confrontation with the Eagle of divine Justice in *Paradiso*, XIX–XX. And nowhere, perhaps, in the *Comedy* is his religion, in the strictest sense of the term, as strikingly manifest as in these cantos. However, for the sake of brevity, I propose to leave this particular topic on one side; another lecture would be required to bring out its implicit connexions with the points I shall be more directly concerned with. But it is not irrelevant to these connexions to observe that the salvation of the 'good pagans' was a personal issue for Dante in a sense which hardly applies to the more strictly philosophical problems already mentioned. For while the latter were common scholastic topics, the former was not; so that its extremely vivid emergence in the *Comedy*, in the figure of Virgil, in the other adult inhabitants of Limbo, and finally in *Par.* XIX–XX is, I think, deeply symptomatic. I would say, too, that it represents a point of transition between the scholastic culture which so largely formed Dante and the humanist culture which followed it and which Dante in some ways— all differences allowed for—prepared and foreshadowed.[1]

The underlying and fundamental issue I want to focus upon was Dante's constant preoccupation with the contrast between temporal and eternal happiness; the problem posed for him, as a believer in survival after death, by the apparently twofold end of human existence. Some such dualism seems implicit in Christianity; but in Dante's mind it was, I think, reinforced both by circumstances (in particular, the death of Beatrice) and by philosophical reflexion. This reflexion was historically conditioned by two main

[1] Cf. G. Toffanin, *Ultimi saggi* (Bologna, 1960), pp. 3–67.

background factors: by the great wave of non-Christian philosophy and science already alluded to; and then by the tradition, long established in the Western Church and recently very impressively exhibited and renewed by men like Albert the Great and Aquinas, that reason and religious belief can and should be in harmony; that in principle they need not disagree, that the burden of proof was on those who said that they did. This optimistic view of the relation between faith and reason prevailed, for the most part, in the West from Augustine to the fourteenth century, and it is generally presupposed in all Dante's mature writings; hints of astral determinism in the *Rime* and the Letters are exceptions to the rule and in any case do not give rise to any opposing of philosophy to faith *in principle*. On the other hand, in his writings prior to the *Comedy*—and among these I include the *Monarchia*, because, though it may have been begun after the *Comedy* was begun, it surely represents, in its general spirit and emphasis, a provisional stage of development—in these writings a concept of philosophy seems to be implied which, while not contradicting the tradition I speak of, is not exactly in line with it either—is at least potentially aberrant and eccentric. What in general I mean by this last phrase will, I hope, become clear in due course. But two signs of what I would call an eccentricity in respect of traditional views may be mentioned at once. They both appear in the *Convivio* and are both symptomatic of the extraordinary philosophical enthusiasm which possessed Dante when writing this treatise; and go to show that at this time he conceived philosophy as quite distinct and autonomous *vis-à-vis* theology. One sign is positive, the other negative. The positive sign is the very unusual (to say the least) way in which he represents the service philosophy can render to the Christian faith. In traditional thinking, philosophy served faith, performed her office of *ancilla theologiae*, by proving certain *prolegomena* to faith (for example the existence of God) and then by clearing up misunderstandings which might hinder growth in the faith (for example a confusion between 'nature' and 'person' in the case of the dogma of the Trinity). But the chief direct *evidence* that supported the act of faith itself, in the traditional view, was not, of course, philosophy but those acts of God which St John called signs and the theologians called miracles. But this did not satisfy Dante. His enthusiasm for Lady Philosophy required that *she* should be the miracle; that if she aided Christianity she did so precisely as a sign and a wonder; and a more effective one indeed than those wrought by Christ, for they belong to the past but *she* is visibly present now: 'for [...] since many persons are so hard to persuade that [...] they doubt those miracles [of Christ] and can believe in none of which they do not have visual experience; and this lady [philosophy] is visibly miraculous [...] it is clear that with the marvel of her countenance this lady aids our faith' (*Con.* iii, vii, 16; cf. xiv, 13–14). And how does she do this? Why, by simply being herself, the intellectual light of this world; for, simply by reducing the strangeness of this natural world to a rational order, philosophy helps us to believe that the strange things proposed for belief by Christianity are themselves rational, and therefore real, from the point of view of 'a higher intellect', namely God's (*ibid.* xiv, 14).

Philosophy has been transferred to the place traditionally assigned to miracle; and this, be it noted, without the slightest explicit allusion to her traditional function as theology's handmaid.[1]

And this brings me to the negative sign. In all the reasoning and rhapsodies about Lady Philosophy in the *Convivio* there is never a hint that she had anything to do with the elaboration of a rational *theology*, as Aquinas, for example, understood theology—as a science which, postulating the truth of Revelation, used natural reason as an aid to understanding it. Set against this Thomist idea of *sacra doctrina* as a tough hard-working collaboration of faith and reason here on earth, how remote and ethereal and...inactive seems theology as Dante depicts it in that curious allegory in *Con.* II (xiii–xiv), which correlates the heavenly spheres and the sciences! To the 'heavens' known to natural reason, from that of the Moon up to the Primum Mobile, correspond, he says, the sciences that compose the 'body' of Lady Philosophy; while to theology, 'la divina scienza' (note the epithet!), Dante leaves only the outermost heaven known to faith alone, the Empyrean, the heaven of utter, motionless peace; for is not theology the utterly peaceful science, unlike the others quite undisturbed by the clash and difference of human opinions? This is not a picture of theology that St Thomas or any other scholastic theologian would have recognized; nor does it in the least resemble the sort of thing Beatrice gives us repeatedly in the *Paradiso* (cantos IV, V, VII, XXVIII and XXIX; compare XIII, XIX, XXIV–XXVI)—hard reasoning from premises supplied by faith.

[1] Cf. E. Gilson, *Dante et la philosophie, op. cit.* pp. 114–22.

And if it had been, at an earlier stage, Dante's idea of theology, this was surely because then all the force and fervour of his intellect were still concentrated on philosophy, the wisdom attainable by the light of reason alone.

Let us try now to get a little closer to that intellectual force and fervour. Dante's first writings were, of course, lyric verse, and I will not delay to tease out such philosophy as this part of his *œuvre* may imply. The *Vita Nuova* (1292–5) shows, along with a keen religious sensibility, some rudiments of a philosophical culture; and we have it from Dante himself (*Con.* II, xii) that it was not until after the death of Beatrice (1290) that he began the serious study of philosophy (which for him included physical science), pushing on from what he already knew of the seven Liberal Arts, the basis of medieval education, to Natural Philosophy, Ethics and Metaphysics. The general lines of this advance were fixed by the Aristotelian division of the sciences, and its conceptual formulation by the Arab and Christian commentators on Aristotle (thus, for example, Dante seems from the first to have read the Nicomachean Ethics in conjunction with St Thomas's commentary). There was, of course, a good deal of Neoplatonist influence mixed in with all this and conveyed more directly by works like the *Liber de Causis* and by Boethius and Cicero. It was indeed from these last two more humane, less technical writers that the initial decisive impulse came. It was, Dante tells us, to console himself for Beatrice's death (*Con.* II, xii), that he began to read 'that little known work' the *Consolatio Philosophiae* and then Cicero on Friendship. At first he found these texts difficult; he was after all already over twenty-five and married, with the distractions of a growing family; but he persevered. And then the decisive experience came. He found he had entered a marvellous new world; real, yet grander than any dream: both translucent and mysterious: an immense unfathomable *order* of parts in a whole, with at its centre a luminous experience which from now on became the deepest spring and motive of his life—the experience of his own mind seeing truth. It cannot be too much emphasized that behind all the close reasoning that plays so large a part in Dante's work from now on, and also, and no less, behind all the dance of his poetic imagination, there was a passionate intuitive experience: an experience at once intellectual (and so potentially philosophical) and emotional (and so potentially poetic). The former, intellectual aspect first emerges clearly after that initial contact with philosophy; the second aspect, engaging the sensibility and emotions, had already of course emerged in the youthful lyric poetry and the *Vita Nuova*; and was to persist as an underglow through the prose works of his middle period—*Convivio, De Vulgari Eloquentia, Monarchia*—and to find its final expression in the *Comedy*. The best formula for the experience itself is perhaps a phrase of St Augustine's: *gaudium de veritate*, the joy of a conscious contact with truth. But what also needs to be stressed is the aspect of *inclusiveness*: I mean that it did not, in one sense, matter to Dante what the particular object of his knowing might be, since the joy of knowing it was already a foretaste of all conceivable knowledge and all joy; and this precisely because, in knowing, the mind seized *truth*. Truth was the proper distinctive aim, the 'good' of the intellect (*Con.* II, xiii, 6; cf. I, i, I; IV, xv, II), and at the touch of truth—whether this came through understanding the beauty of a poem or of a woman, or a proposition in geometry, or variations in the weather, or the virtue of justice, or the motions of the stars—at the touch of any truth whatsoever the whole mind stirred, all its energies awoke. This is to say that for Dante the slightest experience of truth had a cosmic, more exactly a metaphysical, significance: once intelligence, the truth-faculty, had tasted truth as such, that is, its own correspondence with reality, it could not help desiring truth whole and entire, that is, its correspondence with all reality. Hence the great trajectory of intellectual desire sketched at the end of *Paradiso*, IV, between two stages of Beatrice's discourse on the human will (he is addressing her):

> O amanza del primo amante, o diva,
>   diss'io appresso ...
> Io veggio ben che già mai non si sazia
>   nostro intelletto, se 'l ver non lo illustra
>   di fuor dal qual nessun vero si spazia.
> Posasi in esso come fera in lustra,
>   tosto che giunto l'ha; e giugner puollo:
>   se non, ciascun disio sarebbe frustra.
> Nasce per quello, a guisa di rampollo,
>   a pié del vero il dubbio; ed è natura
>   ch'al sommo pinge noi di collo in collo.★

>   (*Par.* IV, 118–32.)

★ 'O beloved of the First Lover, O divine one...I see well that our intellect can never be satisfied except with that truth beyond which no truth extends. There it reposes, like a wild beast in its lair, as soon as it reaches it: and reach it it can, else all desire would be in vain. This is why enquiry springs up like a sapling at the foot of truth—which is nature driving us on from hill to hill.'

Note the word *natura*; latent in human nature itself, and awakened by the *natural* experience of truth, is a desire that cannot ultimately stop short of perfect all-embracing vision, the 'perfetto veder' that Beatrice mentions a few lines on (*Par.* v, 5) and which will in fact be the direct sight of God that terminates the poem. And it is this final vision which has already somehow polarized the poet's 'spirit' and is drawing it on through all the intermediary moments of truth-seeing and the questions ('dubbio') that they breed or 'seed'. And so Beatrice replies (echoing his 'I see well'):

> Io veggio ben sí come già resplende
> ne l'intelletto tuo l'etterna luce
> che, vista, sola e sempre amore accende.*
>
> (*Par.* v, 7–9.)

—lines which the attentive reader will link with what was said of the first vision, in the Earthly Paradise, of Beatrice's unveiled eyes:

> l'anima mia gustava di quel cibo
> che, saziando di sé, di sé asseta.†
>
> (*Purg.* XXXI, 128–9.)

—a clear echo of the phrase in *Ecclesiasticus* (xxiv, 29) about the infinite desirability of divine wisdom: 'Those who eat me shall yet hunger, those who drink of me shall yet thirst.' Tasting truth the mind tastes the food it precisely exists to feed upon (hence the momentary satisfaction, 'saziando di sé') and to feed upon eternally (hence the dissatisfaction, 'di sé asseta').

* 'I see well that the eternal light is already reflected in your mind—the light which, once seen, alone and always kindles love.'

† 'My soul was tasting that food which, even while of itself it satisfies, causes a thirst of itself.'

And such texts can send us back again to the *Convivio*, particularly to that wonderful passage in book IV (xii, 13–20) about the soul's natural desire to return to its 'principio' who is God; and this in turn with its brilliantly sustained image of the soul as a wayfarer, recalls the 'pilgrim' theme that emerged at the end of the *Vita Nuova* (XL–XLI); while in other ways clearly preparing for the lines in *Purg.* XVI (to which Eliot has accustomed English ears), about the soul issuing from the hand of God and turning eagerly to whatever seems to promise delight, just because it comes from One who created it in and with delight:

> Esce di mano a lui che la vagheggia
> prima che sia, a guisa di fanciulla
> che piangendo e ridendo pargoleggia,
> l'anima semplicetta che sa nulla,
> salvo che, mossa da lieto fattore,
> volentier torna a ciò che la trastulla.*
>
> (*Purg.* XVI, 85–90.)

But it will be best if we follow the clue contained in that paradox, in *Purg.* XXXI, of the food that both satisfies and leaves unsatisfied ('saziando di sé, di sé asseta'); for this leads to the centre of my subject. What I hope to show is, first, that Dante's thought about man's relation to God goes in either of two apparently opposite directions according to the point of view he is adopting in a given context or time; and then, secondly, to suggest at least, in conclusion, that there is a point at which the two lines come together.

---

* 'Issues from the hand of Him who loves her before she exists, like a child that plays about weeping and laughing, the simple soul that knows nothing except that, come from a glad maker, she turns willingly to whatever gives her pleasure.'

For it is clear on the one hand (the texts already cited have shown it) that he saw the human soul as so intimately and thoroughly involved, so to say, with God that only an experience of God could satisfy its natural craving; while it is equally clear, as we shall see, that he sometimes stresses very hard—as hard, perhaps, as a professed Christian could —the *distance* between man and God and the at least *pro tempore* sufficiency for man of natural objects and secular concerns. So our problem is that of relating what may loosely be called Dante's humanism with his religion. By his religion one must mean, in the last resort, his Christianity as this finds expression in the *Comedy*. But we should be careful how we introduce the strictly Christian factor when distinguishing those two lines, as I called them, the other-worldly and this-worldly trends in his thought. True, Christianity always meant other-worldliness for Dante; indeed it meant it to a very marked degree: if I had to state in one phrase the distinctively Dantean way of regarding Christianity, I would say that he saw it as the way to eternal vision—with the main stress on vision. On the other hand, his humanism—taking this to mean his assertion of the value of human nature in the scale of being, on the basis of what he at least *thought* was a purely rational analysis—this humanism was not in principle simply this-worldly; it was in principle both this-worldly and other-worldly: other-worldly inasmuch as philosophy alone, without any help from faith or theology, showed that man's reach extended beyond this world; this-worldly inasmuch as it also showed that there was so much for man to know and do in this world that he could be content, and rightly content, to leave that further 'reach' for the time being unexercised. Thus in her own way Lady Philosophy embodies a paradox similar to that presented by the unveiled Beatrice. Both ladies promise satisfaction and bring a dissatisfaction. But, whereas in Beatrice's case the stress falls, however lightly (but compare *Purg.* xxxII, 9), on present dissatisfaction (there is, after all, the whole *Paradiso* yet to come), with Lady Philosophy the stress is reversed; it falls on present satisfaction. In other ways the two ladies are remarkably alike: the stress on the eyes and the smile of Beatrice in *Purg.* xxxI, 118–45, picks up, in fact, and focuses into a few lines of intense poetry an allegory concerning Lady Philosophy which had been laboriously unfolded in the prose of *Con.* III, xv.

The Beatrice who unveils herself in the Earthly Paradise is certainly an allegory too; but what she represents, unlike her partial prototype, is supernatural revealed doctrine, Christian wisdom: the object her eyes are mirroring is the *animal binato*, the two-natured Gryphon, symbol of the God-Man, Christ: hence the vision Dante is now granted of her eyes and smile, here in the Earthly Paradise, is a foretaste of the Celestial Paradise which he will soon enter. But this is to place it within the consciously Christian scheme of the *Comedy*; whereas, considered simply as an *experience*, it is hardly distinguishable from the natural experience of the philosopher as described in the *Convivio*. Here, according to the allegory, the eyes of Lady Philosophy are 'proofs' ('demonstrazioni') in which reason sees truth with certitude; while her smile stands for certain 'intimations' ('persuasioni') through which reason—the same natural reason—has a *chiaroscuro* perception of certain deeper truths glimpsed under a sort of veil ('sotto alcuno velamento'). Together the eyes and the smile represent all the wisdom attainable by man on earth. Clearly, it is a limited wisdom, as the distinction between proofs and intimations implies; the limitation, as Dante goes on to explain (*Con.* III, xv, 6; compare iv, 9; IV, xiii, 7; xxii, 13), consisting in man's inability to understand 'certain things' which he nevertheless knows to exist—God and angels and *la prima materia*. And yet—and here is the crucial point— this purely natural wisdom involves an experience which in its own way is completely satisfying, since it terminates, if only momentarily, the essential human desire, the inborn drive of the rational soul to the act of understanding. This is the act proper to the human soul *qua* human, and so it brings man to the peace or contentment proper to him, and in this sense is final and absolute (*Con.* III, xv, 3–5). But what else is the bliss of Paradise but a final and absolute contentment? The only difference then, from *this* point of view, is that the paradisal bliss goes on forever whereas the bliss of truth-seeing on earth does not.

Let us examine a little the implications of this way of representing philosophy and the philosophical life. We have to note in the first place that Dante did not draw his idea or, better, his ideal of philosophy (as distinct from his philosophical tools and equipment) only from the Aristotelian tradition, even as supplemented by Neoplatonist sources. He drew it also from the Bible, from the Sapiential books of the Vulgate Old Testament: indeed it was the description of divine wisdom in *Proverbs* VIII and

Wisdom VIII–IX—texts which he never wearies of citing —that gave him his favourite image of the ideal. This divine wisdom he conceived as the supreme type and exemplar of philosophy itself; and this because, through its identity with the divine essence, it answered exactly to his full definition of philosophy as perfectly realized— namely, as a love of wisdom actually and fully possessed, perfectly under one's control: 'filosofia è uno amoroso uso di sapienza' (*Con.* III, xii, 12), where 'uso' connotes full possession and 'sapienza' has its objective sense of 'what a philosopher knows'—which for Dante was potentially everything, the entire range of being, since intellect was the capacity for truth as such and truth (in the tradition he followed) was coterminous with being, *verum et ens convertuntur*. In God, where truth and being are identical, intellection is necessarily eternal, and philosophy therefore at its highest perfection: it is like 'an eternal marriage' of mind and wisdom. This cannot be the case in created intellects, angelic or human; in these wisdom is more like a mistress than a wife: 'quasi come druda de la quale nullo amadore prende compiuta gioia, ma nel suo aspetto contentan la loro vaghezza'* (*Con.* III, xii, 13). The imperfection, then, consists in not possessing wisdom completely; and this in man (not in the angels) shows itself as an intermittency, a discontinuity in actual understanding. Thus degrees of intelligence in Dante's scale of being are measured by approximation to the condition of eternity; and human limitation is seen primarily as subjection to

* 'Like a mistress from whom none of her lovers gets complete joy, but in the sight of whom their desires are brought to rest.'

time. Nevertheless intelligence (or mind) and the correlative terms wisdom and philosophy always and at all levels connote something divine, for their ultimate measure and exemplar is God. And their presence in man means that man—and still with respect to his *nature*, quite apart from supernatural grace—is in some sense divine (compare *Con.* III, ii, 14, 19); but with a 'divinity' that is only intermittently actual and apparent.

So a contrast appears between an inborn 'divinity' in man, due to his share in intelligence, and the actual conditions of human life in the body and in time. The classic statement of this theme, for the Middle Ages and Dante, was Aristotle's remark in book x of the *Ethics*, that a life given up wholly to intellectual speculation would transcend the human condition, since 'not in so far as man is man would he live it, but in so far as there is something divine in him' (*Nic. Eth.* x, 7: 1177 b 26–30). Potentially at any rate, then, the intellectual life is superhuman; and superhuman too, then, is its perfect bliss and fulfilment in an uninterrupted, unending contemplation of truth. And this is the idea behind the distinction that Dante now begins to draw, with increasing emphasis, through book IV of the *Convivio*, and which is implied throughout the *Monarchia*, between the active and the contemplative lives. The distinction was traditional but he drew it in a very personal way. Briefly, one might say that he now tends—especially in writings other than the *Comedy*, but the tendency left traces in the *Comedy* too—to regard human life, properly speaking, as a life directed to ends attainable on earth, and to relegate to a life after death the whole possibility and

67   5-2

process of man's divinization (the *trasumanar*, as he will call it in *Par.* 1, 70). As a Christian Dante could not, even in his most secular moments, conceive of the process of divinization apart from some intervention of divine grace (and, to start with, apart from the Incarnation); but he shows an inclination—even, I would say, in the *Comedy*—very closely to associate the intervention of grace with the passage from mortality to immortality. So far as this tendency can be identified with his general bias to regarding Christianity *primarily* as the way to eternal vision (a bias I feel through all Dante's work, from *Vita Nuova* to *Paradiso*) it is not as such unorthodox; but a risk of heresy did, I think, in fact come in, inasmuch as, following that bias, he rather tended to resolve the theologian's distinction between nature and grace into a philosopher's distinction between time and eternity.

To bring this point out more clearly let us turn again to *Con.* III, xv; which in turn will lead us to the great concluding chapter of the *Monarchia*, the chief single statement of the Dantean view of man outside the *Comedy*. We shall find, I think, Dante pressing his distinction between the earthly and the heavenly ends of man so far as almost to identify life on earth with *human* life proper, and to seem almost to leave in abeyance, so far as man *qua* man is concerned, any connexion with a life after death.

We have heard Dante say, it will be recalled, that the eyes and the smile of philosophy can give man, even here on earth, a quasi-complete happiness; the eyes being philosophy's 'proofs' and the smile certain intimations of things that remain for the time being half-veiled. But then, very naturally, he raises the question how this half-knowledge is compatible with that quasi-paradisal happiness—'since man naturally desires to know, and as long as this desire is unfulfilled he cannot be happy'. Briefly, his answer is that every natural desire—the desire in everything for its proper perfection—is conditioned by possibility; nothing *naturally* desires the impossible. Therefore in this life the natural desire of the intellect is limited to what it can see in this life; and since it can see something (whether as proved or merely intimated) it can here and now be satisfied: 'And so human desire is measured in this life by the knowledge humanly possible in this life...and therefore, since it is not possible to our nature to know what God and certain other things *are*, we do not naturally desire such knowledge' (*Con.* iii, xv, 10). This answer may seem facile, but let us look more closely. It is plain, of course, that the expression 'human desire' is used here, not absolutely, but relatively to life on earth, in the body. On the other hand, we shall not, I think, press the text too hard if we understand it to say that the possibilities that here and now condition the 'human desire' are imposed by *human nature itself*—note how unqualified is the statement that a certain knowledge of God is impossible *a la nostra natura*. From which it seems to follow that any *further* desire—any natural desire to see the divine essence as such—must pertain to a nature *other than human*. And since Dante certainly believed in the immortality of the soul, and saw it as the condition of the intellect's reaching entire and absolute satisfaction (compare *Con.* iv, xxii, 13–18), then, from the point of view he is at present adopting, he is placing the soul after death outside human nature proper —as he says elsewhere, after death the soul lives on in 'natura più che umana' (*ibid.* II, viii, 6). For *human* nature there is life on earth; a life to be directed therefore to a strictly human end—Aristotle's τὸ ἀγαθὸν ἀνθρώπινον— to be achieved by strictly human means, the exercise of human virtue, ἡ ἀρετὴ ἀνθρωπίνη (*Nic. Eth.* I, 13, 1102a 14–15).

A comparison with St Thomas may help here. St Thomas would not have agreed that the soul after death was, strictly speaking, 'in natura più che umana'; but he might, I think, have considered that on this point at least the difference between himself and Dante was perhaps more verbal than real. Both start from the Aristotelian position that both soul and body are essential components of human nature. The chief difficulty that this raised for Aquinas, with regard to the soul after death, was how the soul could *know* anything after separation from the bodily senses on which its knowledge naturally depended. He could have dodged the difficulty by invoking the supernatural power of God; but he was not the man to use miraculous short-cuts. Alternatively he might have said: Of course the soul can know after death, and in fact better than before—its union with a body is only extraneous and incidental. But this would have been to slip back into Platonism. His solution was to say that the 'separated' soul, while remaining the same in nature, took on a different kind of existence, *alius modus essendi*, which was somehow not in keeping with its nature: *esse separatam a corpore est praeter rationem suae naturae* (*Summa theol.* 1a.89.1).

But the point to be stressed is his concern all through the discussion to avoid being drawn back into Platonism by the doctrine of immortality—to maintain this doctrine and still be an integral Aristotelian. Dante's concern was quite different; it was much more moral than metaphysical. Combining a roughly Aristotelian position as to the union of soul and body in man with the Philosopher's remark in *Ethics*, x, 7, that a purely intellectual life would be more than human, Dante either drew, or came very near to drawing, the conclusion that only while soul and body are conjoined is there human nature at all. And he did this not, I think, as compelled by any strict analysis, but mainly for the practical reason that he wanted to assert very strongly the validity of the proximate, this-worldly ends of human activity. He was no doubt led to this chiefly by his intense concern with individual and social ethics, the concern that glows through the moral canzoni of the decade 1294–1305 and the fourth book of the *Convivio* (1306–8). And doubtless two other factors played their part: the extraordinary vividness of his immediate intellectual experiences as a philosopher in this world; and then, in apparent contrast with that, but in fact combining with it to focus attention on terrestrial objects and concerns (in the field of ethics and politics), a deep sense of the littleness and insufficiency of human metaphysics.[1]

This secular, this-worldly aspect of Dante's mind comes to its sharpest focus in the *Monarchia*. The stress here falls entirely on finite ends and secondary causes. One can feel it immediately in the prominence given the term *natura* in

[1] On this point see E. Gilson, *op. cit.* pp. 122–30.

the treatise, as denoting the whole system of secondary, physical causes (epitomized as 'the heavens', *coelum*) on which terrestrial life depends. Each of the three books starts with an axiom in praise of *natura*. By contrast, God is remote, acting only at a remove—except, and this of course is crucial, inasmuch as he directly confers authority on both emperor and pope. From the special standpoint of the *Monarchia* God is simply the *a priori* condition of the workings of Nature and the authority of institutions—and of the natural institution, the Empire, in the first place. By the Empire Dante meant a world-monarchy which, by ensuring peace on earth, would enable mankind to fulfil its earthly destiny, and so enjoy all the happiness possible to man on earth and in time. But the realization of this ideal was hindered by the Church: in practice by intrusions into the sphere of civil government; at the speculative level by the theory, upheld in papal documents and canon law, that the civil power received its authority and jurisdiction from God indeed, but only as mediated through the Church. It was to refute this theory that Dante wrote *Mon.* iii; but only in the concluding chapter (xvi) does his basic principle emerge quite clearly, in an extremely definite statement of the position we have seen him hinting at and groping towards in the *Convivio*. Man alone among all beings is both mortal and immortal; mortal by his body, immortal by the rational soul. Soul and body are both of the 'essence' of man; nevertheless, since each is reducible to a different kind of 'nature'—the one to that of things incorruptible, the other to that of things corruptible—and since every nature has its own distinctive ultimate end (*cum omnis natura ad ultimum quendam finem ordinetur*), it follows that man—and he alone in all the universe—has *two* ultimate ends (*duplex finis: duo ultima*), namely temporal felicity in this world and eternal felicity after death. And in what does each felicity consist? We are already prepared for Dante's answer by the distinction noted above (and which, I repeat, he drew chiefly from Aristotle) between the active life in the autonomous exercise of human virtue —a life therefore characteristically human—and the contemplative life in the exercise of pure intellect, which is characteristically 'divine'. All that Dante adds here is an allusion to God's helping grace as the pre-condition of the ascent from mortal to immortal life (an allusion required by the context which is all a marking out of the boundaries between 'nature' and 'supernature'):

Ineffable Providence, then, has set before man two ends at which he should aim: Happiness in this life, which consists in exercising his own specific capacity (*que in operatione proprie virtutis consistit*) and is symbolized in the earthly Paradise; and happiness in eternal life, which consists in enjoying the divine beauty, to which enjoyment man's own capacity cannot attain unless it be aided by a divine light; and this happiness is what is meant by the heavenly Paradise (III, xvi, 3–7).

This, for my purpose, is all I need cite from the *Monarchia*; the essential point was contained in the phrase *duo ultima*—man has two ultimate ends. We have seen how the *Convivio* (certainly written earlier) can prepare us for such a statement. I have laid less stress on—though I have not ignored—passages which run counter to it, which speak of man's inborn desire to re-unite with God—an end in respect of which no other end could be regarded, ultimately, except as a means; so that, from this point of view, Dante's effort in the *Monarchia* to distinguish two 'natures' within the one human 'essence' may seem almost like verbal juggling—or anyhow like calling in dubious metaphysics to justify an ethico-political commitment. And yet, once stated, how glib this formula sounds! If a formula is required, let me call the *Monarchia* the most direct, concentrated and complete expression of one of the deepest elements in Dante's complex nature, his devotion to the idea of human solidarity in the political community, his sense of being involved with his fellow men in the common pursuit of a common good on earth. But he had always a sense too of a still deeper, if not always so intensely felt, involvement—that implied in being, quite simply, a creature, involved with all things, stones and stars and fellow men and angels, in a common relationship to the Creator. And this deeper theme still awaited his genius.

It is, however, at least imaginable that the course of Dante's development might have stopped at an *impasse*. There may be no difference in principle between the *Monarchia* and the *Comedy*; but a difference of 'slant', emphasis, perspective, there undoubtedly is: enough to repeat that the one work looks wholly to temporal existence, the other to eternal. It does not follow, of course, that the *Monarchia* is simply an irreligious work, if by religion one means only a general reverence towards a felt 'divinity' in things; for there is certainly *that* in the *Monarchia*. But, more strictly, religion can mean trying to get as close as possible to that 'divinity', whatever it may

be; it means seeking God, in short; and to see Dante really
seeking God we have to turn to the *Comedy*. I must
not, in the little time left to me, attempt to follow him on
that search. All I shall, in conclusion, attempt is to suggest
an explanation of his having started out on the search at
all—I mean, of course, the search as expressed in the poem.

The Japanese sage Shimai Soshitsu told his pupils: 'It is
forbidden to worry about the after-life until one has reached
the age of fifty.' Dante was certainly not so old when he
began the *Comedy*; and if the works of his youth hardly
show him worrying about the after-life, the *Vita Nuova*
clearly shows him already thinking about heaven:

> Oltre la spera che più larga gira
> passa 'l sospiro ch'esce del mio core ...*

The sonnet I quote from, at the close of the *Vita Nuova*
(XLI, 10–13), a straw in the wind, already shows, to our
hindsight, the direction in which the poet was ultimately
to go. Indeed it is not, I think, fanciful to take it as the
expression of, in this respect, a germinal experience: I find
it at any rate more plausible to trace the *Comedy* back to an
idea of heaven than to an idea of hell; and therefore,
inevitably, to trace it back to Beatrice—to an adolescent's
association of a girl's beauty with God's, and of human love
with a desire that had to reach beyond the grave to find
fulfilment. All through Dante's *œuvre* the idea of eternal
life, and bliss, is inseparable from Beatrice; she functions
all through as a sort of epitome of his interest in it. In the
Vita Nuova her heaven-showing function is clear:

* 'Beyond the widest-circling sphere passes the sigh that comes from
my heart.'

e par che sia una cosa venuta
da cielo in terra a miracol mostrare.★

(*VN*, xxvi, son. *Tanto gentile*.)

and when she dies she naturally returns to heaven, followed
by Dante's love as a 'pilgrim spirit'. And when, in the
middle period that followed, Dante's thoughts turned
mainly to this world, bent on aims to be achieved, Aristo-
telianly, here and now, then naturally Beatrice retired from
the scene—bowed out courteously from the *Convivio* (ii,
viii, 7) and of course absent from the *Monarchia*. 'The
Virgil of the *Monarchia* expects no Beatrice', said Giovanni
Gentile, and the remark is not as foolish as Gilson sup-
posed.[1] But of course in the *Comedy* Virgil *does* expect her;
more important, she expects him; for it is she who sends
him—Virgil, in the prose treatise only the prophet of an
earthly kingdom (*Mon.* i, xi, 1; ii, iii, 6, etc.)—to save
Dante by leading him towards the heavenly one, with
which she had been poetically identified at the close of the
Vita Nuova. About Dante's state of mind on beginning the
Comedy one inference at least is surely valid: that he was
deliberately starting from the point where he had left off
in his youth. It was in some sense a return to Beatrice.

But why exactly did he return? Well, for the most part
one can only conjecture. External circumstances played
their part, no doubt: the collapse of his hopes of returning
to Florence, the rise or collapse of his hope of seeing the
Empire restored by Henry of Luxembourg. Who can

[1] Quoted by B. Nardi, *Saggi di filosofia dantesca* (Milan, 1930), p. 304;
cf. Gilson, *op. cit.* pp. 163–4.

★ 'She seems a thing come from heaven to earth to make a marvel
visible.'

say exactly how far such things occasioned the poem? The suggestions I would offer have to do, rather, with pressures from within, with impulses arising from principles long cherished and from a personal judgement passed on himself by his own conscience. To be more plain, I suggest that one main motive setting him to work on the *Comedy* was that he wished once and for all to give full attention to, bring all his powers of thought, imagination and poetic construction to bear on, the theme of man's radical orientation to God, as a being impelled by nature to find his happiness in discovering the *raison-d'être* of his existence; and I suggest, as a second main motive, some *crise de conscience*, some fresh realization that came to Dante in middle age that he was a sinner in need of forgiveness. Of these two suggested motives the second would be the more specifically Christian, perhaps; and, in that sense, for Dante the more religious. But I hope it will be enough, by way of relating it to the *Comedy*, to refer simply to *Purg.* xxx–xxxiii. The other motive, the concern with God as the final object of desire, is as such independent of a sense of sin or any precisely moral crisis. Yet the intensity and range of its expression in the *Comedy* strongly suggest—with the *Monarchia* and the other texts already examined in mind—some very personal crisis undergone by the poet in this respect as well; a certain shift towards the real and the concrete; a certain refusal any longer to compromise, even with Aristotelian justifications; a decision that it was not after all as important as it had once seemed to distinguish man as man from man as potentially divine; a mounting sense of the desperate brevity of this life—'di quella vita che al termine vola'—where so much could be begun, so little completed; and where, in any case, every effort, every momentary desire however apparently trivial had behind it the force of an absolutely basic initial desire for God—a desire springing from the original creative act itself which had brought the soul into existence:

> 'ma vostra vita sanza mezzo spira
>   la somma beninanza, e la innamora
>   di sé sì che poi sempre la disira.'*
>
> (*Par.* VII, 142–4.)

And this natural desire is, in effect, a desire for divine grace, for a life beyond the limits of nature, made available to man by the Incarnation:

> La sete natural che mai non sazia
>   se non con l'acqua onde la femminetta
>   sammaritana dimandò la grazia....†
>
> (*Purg.* XXI, 1–3.)

---

* 'But your life the supreme Goodness breathes forth without any intermediary, and he so enamours it of himself that it then always desires him.'

† 'The natural thirst which nothing slakes except the water the Samaritan woman asked for.' The allusion is, of course, to John IV, 10–15.

4

DANTE'S LYRIC POETRY

P. BOYDE

It was to the composition of lyric poetry that Dante devoted the whole of the first half of his creative life. From the age of eighteen to thirty-eight (1283–1303) he seems to have written nothing else, and even in the years immediately following (1303–8) he apparently still re-garded his lyric poetry as pre-eminent. For he continued to write poems—even if only a handful—in this period, and the two uncompleted prose works with which he was principally occupied were—in theory at least—subordinate to his poetry. All the linguistic theory and information in the *De Vulgari Eloquentia* is only in preparation for its detailed instructions and advice about the writing of *canzoni*, whilst the *Convivio* takes the form of a detailed commentary on three of his *canzoni*.

What survives of this twenty and more years' activity? In the opinion of Barbi, the editor of the relevant sections of the critical text, there are 88 poems which can be attrib-uted to Dante beyond reasonable doubt. These comprise 59 sonnets, 6 *ballate* and 23 *canzoni*. To these we must add many narrative or descriptive passages in the prose of the *Vita Nuova* (composed *c.* 1292–5), which as we shall see share one inspiration with the poems, and indeed the *Vita Nuova* considered as a whole, as an individual work of art, and not just as an anthology of poems with the author's annotations. For the *Vita Nuova*, unlike the *De Vulgari Eloquentia*, is not a book *about* poetry: it is a book *of* poetry. In essence indeed it is a poem, Dante's greatest poem before the *Comedy*. On no account is it to be studied outside the context of his lyric poetry, and no survey of that poetry which ignores the work can be complete.

Eighty-eight poems and the prose of the *Vita Nuova* may not seem much to show for twenty years' work. It should be remembered however that quite a number of Dante's poems may not have come down to us (he himself mentions two lost poems in his prose works); that he may be the author of some of the thirty poems classified by Barbi as *Rime dubbie*; and that he might even be the author of *Il Fiore*, a free adaptation of the *Roman de la Rose* in a cycle of 232 sonnets. But in any case there is no need to call on such dubious allies: the authenticated work is sufficient in itself to establish Dante as the greatest Italian lyric poet of the thirteenth century.

There are two main periods in Dante's career as a lyric poet, and, conveniently enough, each lasted more or less exactly ten years, and each was terminated by prose works that describe and interpret the main preoccupations and the principal lines of development in the preceding decade.

In the first phase Dante wrote only on themes in some way pertaining to love—'sopra matera amorosa' (*VN*, xxv, 6). Not just on any kind of love, of course, but that which had been professed and to some extent codified by 'courtly' poets over the preceding 200 years. A human and heterosexual love that shunned particularity and everyday reality and was outside or without reference to marriage; a stylized and idealized fiction, with prescribed roles and attitudes for the protagonists; a love which was eternal courtship of a superior being, and which, while it remained such, was a force ennobling the lover and the source of his merit, worth and joy. At first Dante assimilated more or less passively this framework of ideas, situations and themes, and the language, style and forms in which they found expression. Witness the opening of this isolated *canzone* stanza:

> Lo meo servente core
> vi raccomandi Amor, che vi l'ha dato,
> e Merzé d'altro lato
> di me vi rechi alcuna rimembranza;
> ché del vostro valore
> avanti ch'io mi sia guari allungato,
> mi tien già confortato
> di ritornar la mia dolce speranza.★
>
> (*Rime*, XLIX, 1–8.)

But Dante's was a restless and exploring spirit from the beginning, and by the end of this first decade he had developed and refined the traditional concept of love until it almost escapes recognition. We shall have more to say of these 'discoveries' later; for the moment let us pass on to note the parallel development in his style. This is no less striking although it was rather more of a communal achievement. During this decade Guido Cavalcanti, Dante and other friends succeeded in distilling a new style for love poetry. Their vocabulary became more restricted and

★ 'Let Love commend to you my loyal heart—Love who gave it to you; and may Kindness, on your other side, remind you sometimes of me: for now, even before I'm far away from your goodness, already a sweet hope of returning consoles me.'

purer, more truly and consistently elevated than that of their immediate predecessors; their syntax became simpler. They avoided or made sparing use of the many rhetorical *ornatus* in which earlier poets had delighted. For their expressive effects they relied almost exclusively on the natural, effortless grace of their utterances, and, above all, on their music. One still cannot find better epithets for the following lines than those habitually used by Dante to characterize the new style—*dolce* and *soave*:

> Ogne dolcezza, ogne pensero umile
> nasce nel core a chi parlar la sente,
> ond'è laudato chi prima la vide.
> Quel ch'ella par quando un poco sorride,
> non si pò dicer né tenere a mente,
> sì è novo miracolo e gentile.★
>
> (*Rime*, xvii; *VN*, xxi.)

The first decade, then, saw far reaching developments in both the theme and style of love poetry, but the poems nevertheless remain relatively homogeneous. Dante did not have to do great violence to the essential facts when he reinterpreted and recast his experiences in poetic form to produce a work of such perfect unity as the *Vita Nuova*. In the poems of the second decade, and in the half-dozen written after 1303, there is no such unity either in themes or style. The 'sweet style' was still used at first to celebrate —allegorically—Dante's new love for philosophy. But that style had been created to express a particular vision of

---

★ 'All gentleness, every humble thought is born in the heart of all who hear her speak; and so he who first sees her is praised. What she seems when she smiles a little can neither be described nor held before the mind, it is a marvel so rare and perfect.'

love, and, whether we look at it in medieval or modern terms, it was appropriate to that alone. It was in any case an instrument too limited in compass, in dynamic range and in tone-colour to have done justice to the kind of themes to which Dante was now attracted. And so when he felt the urge to expound philosophy—in the form of two long *canzoni* on ethical themes—he deliberately and avowedly laid aside his youthful style, and grappled with his subject in a harsher and more muscular way.

> Le dolci rime d'amor ch' i' solia
> cercar ne' miei pensieri,
> convien ch'io lasci; non perch'io non speri
> ad esse ritornare,
> ma perché li atti disdegnosi e feri,
> che ne la donna mia
> sono appariti, m'han chiusa la via
> de l'usato parlare.*   (*Rime*, LXXXII; *Con.* IV.)

In the years before his exile he made a brief but brilliant excursion into the very different world of the so-called 'comic' or 'low' style, exchanging some abusive sonnets with Forese Donati. And he also gave expression to a violent, sensual love for a *donna petra* in four extrovert and experimental poems which are a kind of homage to the Provençal master of the *trobar ric*, Arnaut Daniel: poems which in the virtuoso handling of rhyme-words and rare rhymes, and in the expressive use of a concrete vocabulary, stand at the antipodes to the love poems of the first decade. After his exile (early in 1302) came two more long poems

---

* 'The sweet love-poetry I was accustomed to seek out in my thoughts I must now forsake; not that I do not hope to return to it, but the proud hard bearing that has become apparent in my lady has barred the path of my usual speech.'

on ethical themes, very different in style and treatment from each other and from the earlier pair, and also some extraordinary correspondence sonnets addressed to Cino da Pistoia.

The two prose works that follow help us to isolate the most important elements in this multifarious production (and it should be noted that I have touched only on the more significant poems). First, the choice of ethical themes: it was the content of his 'philosophical' poems that Dante chose to expound in the *Convivio*, and it is as a poet of *rectitudo*, not *amor*, that he presents himself in the *De Vulgari Eloquentia* (II, ii, 9). Secondly, Dante's ambition to achieve complete mastery of his craft, his preoccupation with technique almost for its own sake: here, the theory of the *De Vulgari* complements and crowns the practical experiments of the preceding years. But even when we have perceived these unifying factors it remains true that the poems of the second decade are disparate, and that they have only a loose connexion with the earlier poems and the *Vita Nuova*.

It will be clear even from such a short sketch that Dante's lyric *opus* does not lend itself readily to any attempt to characterize and illuminate it as a whole. The difficulties fall, I think, into three main categories, and, although I do not propose to take up the challenges they offer, it is relevant to indicate what they are and how they might be met. First, there is the enormous variety and hence dis-unity of the work. Since the only unifying principle seems to be that of growth or development, it becomes almost impossible *not* to study the poems in their known or presumed chronological order, focusing attention on the innovations in style and matter. The second difficulty is that these poems grow out of and remain faithful to a long-lived, sophisticated and ultra-conservative poetic tradition, which in effect dictated both theme and treatment, and in which 'imitation' was regarded as a virtue rather than a vice. All Dante's poems are 'derivative', but very few of them—perhaps a dozen among the earliest—are entirely 'derived'. But the non-specialist reader, even when he has found his general bearings in the field, usually requires help, through a comparison of some of Dante's poems with their models or analogues, before he can make the vital discrimination between the elements that are common and received, and this variation or that departure which give most of the poems a genuine, if always limited, originality. Finally, there is the related difficulty that Dante was a medieval poet writing for an audience of connoisseurs whose assumptions about poetry differed considerably from those current today. The modern reader will look almost in vain for the telling personal phrase, the frequent and original use of metaphor, or the '"concreteness" of texture—the evocation or recreation in words of sensory perceptions and bodily movements'.[1] Instead he must be led to acquire a sympathetic understanding of the rhetorical conception of poetry and expressive language, to learn something of medieval stylistic doctrine, to seek aesthetic satisfaction in the *dolcezza* and *armonia* of the verse, in the rich resources of rhyme, in the artistic structure

[1] This is 'what is especially sought after in literature' today in the opinion of A. C. Spearing, *Criticism and Medieval Poetry* (London, 1964), p. 1.

of the strophe. In a word, he must be shown what Dante meant when he said that poetry was 'nothing other than a work composed in accordance with the canons of rhetoric and music': 'nichil aliud quam fictio rethorica musicaque poita' (*DVE*, II, iv, 2).

It must, however, suffice to have noted these characteristics of Dante's lyric poetry, the problems that they raise, and possible approaches to them.[1] For although the kinds of study suggested are all necessary for a full appreciation of these poems, they all have the disadvantage that they tend to make one ignore the poems as individual works of art, successful or less successful as the case may be. Thus they beg the fundamental question whether or not the poems are good enough to justify the kind of preparatory study they are said to need. Do they in fact offer more than the chance to become familiar with another technique, or to study the evolution of a great poet? These questions are not answered directly in what follows; but I have borne them in mind, and, in general, my aim will be to point to some of the qualities that would lead me to answer that many of the poems are good by any relevant standard, and do demand our attention in their own right.

What is an embarrassment to the critic may prove a source of delight to the reader. And so it is with the great variety found in Dante's poems. For if we come to each

[1] The best available account of the tradition in English is that by M. Valency, *In Praise of Love* (Macmillan Paper Backs, 1961). The other points are fully discussed in the commentary by K. Foster and P. Boyde to their edition of all Dante's poems (Oxford University Press) which will appear in 1966. The translations from Dante's poems are taken from this edition.

poem without preconceptions and ready to accept it on its own terms, we shall find many quite different things to enjoy, frequent and pleasant surprises that do much to compensate for the lack of unity, the absence of a single, more personal voice. Such surprises may be lurking in the most unlikely places. For example, Dante sent one of his poems to an acquaintance, and, as was the pleasant custom of the day, he wrote a sonnet to accompany the gift. It was hardly a propitious occasion for poetry, and obviously we must not expect too much of it:

> Messer Brunetto, questa pulzelletta
> con esso voi si ven la pasqua a fare:
> non intendete pasqua di mangiare,
> ch'ella non mangia, anzi vuol esser letta.
> La sua sentenzia non richiede fretta,
> né luogo di romor né da giullare;
> anzi si vuol più volte lusingare
> prima che 'n intelletto altrui si metta.
>
>   Se voi non la intendete in questa guisa,
> in vostra gente ha molti frati Alberti
> da intender ciò ch'è posto loro in mano.
> Con lor vi restringete sanza risa;
> e se li altri de' dubbi non son certi,
> ricorrete a la fine a messer Giano.★   (*Rime*, xcix.)

At first we are possibly struck by the colloquial ease, the

★ 'Messer Brunetto, this young girl comes to keep Easter with you; not, you understand, an eating Easter, for she doesn't eat, she is meant to be read. Her meaning doesn't call for hasty reading or a place that's noisy, or where players perform; in fact she'll require to be coaxed more than once before she'll enter a man's understanding.

And if you don't understand her in this way, there are many brother Alberts in your company to understand whatever's put into their hands. Get together with them, but without laughing; and if none of them are clear about the difficult bits, in the last resort go and ask Messer Giano.'

lightness of touch so perfectly appropriate to the occasion; by the charm of the affectionate diminutive 'pulzelletta', giving life to the not uncommon personification of the accompanying poem; by the elegance of 'lusingare' or 'mettersi in intelletto altrui' at the close of the octet. But then we notice that, most unusually, the poem is an exquisitely ironical and really very malicious portrait of the recipient and his friends. Reading between the lines we can see that Dante considered them a noisy rabble, fond of the fleshpots, devotees of 'pop' entertainment, doubtless convinced of their own cleverness and scintillating wit but too stupid to make any sense of a poem by Dante. All these traits emerge from the apparently innocuous negative injunctions—'don't jump to the conclusion that it's a gift of food; don't just skim through it once; don't try and read it in your normal stamping grounds': and then in the ironical positive advice—'go into conference with your friends if necessary (but mind, no guffaws); and if those polymaths can't sort out all the tricky bits, well, you can always go and ask Messer Giano'—who was plainly famous either as a simpleton or an obscurantist. In the economy, the control of tone, in the way in which fatal wounds are inflicted with a smile, in the complete transformation of a trivial commonplace, we have something which is not a great poem, but is a *jeu d'esprit* by a considerable poet.

Now let us examine a poem of a totally different kind: rich, elevated, figurative, sententious. It is among the last of the fairly numerous correspondence sonnets that Dante composed at all stages of his career, and since it is the answer to a question relating to 'courtly' love, and since convention required that the reply should follow not only the rhyme scheme but the rhyme sounds of the request-sonnet, we may well come to it with a sinking heart. Cino da Pistoia had asked Dante to confirm his own opinion that— contrary to the absolute fidelity normally prescribed—a man may transfer his affections from one woman to another if there is no hope of his love being requited. Cino demonstrated his own technical competence by using rather uncommon rhyme sounds—'ona', 'eme', 'estra', 'anco'— and this obviously put Dante on his mettle. Here is his reply:

> Io sono stato con Amore insieme
> da la circulazion del sol mia nona,
> e so com'egli affrena e come sprona
> e come sotto lui si ride e geme.
> Chi ragione o virtù contra gli sprieme,
> fa come que' che 'n la tempesta sona,
> credendo far colà dove si tona
> esser le guerre de' vapori sceme.
>
> Però nel cerchio de la sua palestra
> liber arbitrio già mai non fu franco,
> sì che consiglio invan vi si balestra.
> Ben può con nuovi spron punger lo fianco,
> e qual che sia 'l piacer ch'ora n'addestra,
> seguitar si convien, se l'altro è stanco.* (*Rime*, CXI.)

It is a staggering poem from every point of view—not

* 'I have been together with Love since my ninth revolution of the sun, and I know how he curbs and spurs, and how under his sway one laughs and groans. He who urges reason or virtue against him acts like one who raises his voice in a storm, thinking so to lessen the conflict of the clouds, there where the thunder rolls.

Thus within his arena's bounds free will was never free, so that counsel looses its shafts in vain there. Love can indeed prick the flank with new spurs; and whatever the attraction may be that is now leading us, follow we must, if the other one is outworn.'

least from the nature of the sentiments expressed in lines 5–6 and 9–11, at a date which cannot be so remote from the composition of *Inferno* v. Dante moves with complete freedom within the terrible straitjacket of the form, even though he has clearly set out to give Cino a lesson in his craft. Consider the words in rhyme. Those in '-ona' are perhaps no more than enterprising, but those in '-eme' and '-estra' are absolutely dazzling. Yet the poem is perfectly intelligible; and the magisterial tone is maintained without faltering from the arresting opening to the close. The imagery, too, is coherent even though the metaphors must have been largely dictated by the rare words in rhyme. Thus the astronomic periphrasis for 'year'—'circulazion del sol'— prepares us for the meteorological imagery of the second quatrain. 'Le guerre de' vapori'—a phrase at once poetically evocative and scientifically precise, in that thunder was then believed to be caused by the collision of dry and moist exhalations—leads naturally into the combative metaphors of the first tercet, whilst the equestrian image of the close echoes that implicit in the third and fourth lines.

A sonnet like this is of course open to attack on the grounds that it is an interesting display of verbal dexterity and nothing more. It is on the face of it a reasonable charge: but we should beware of pronouncing Dante 'guilty' too hastily. For, as Contini has pointed out,[1] Dante had a taste for the difficult; and a formidable technical challenge often spurred him on to give a truly poetic response. No-

---

[1] Dante Alighieri, *Rime*, ed. G. Contini (Turin, 2nd ed., 1946), *Introduzione*, p. 12. My whole essay is deeply indebted to this brilliant introduction.

where is this more obvious in the lyric poetry than in the *canzoni* written for the 'donna petra'. In each of these Dante has grappled with formal obstacles that would have reduced a lesser man to silence, or at least extinguished any spark of poetry. But, in the first place, Dante will not allow us to make any facile distinction between the form and the content, since he has made the form part of the poem. Thus in the *sestina*, *Al poco giorno* (*Rime*, CI), the recurrence of the same six rhyme-words in every stanza serves to express the obsessive immobility of this love; whilst in the *canzone*, *Così nel mio parlar voglio esser aspro* (*Rime*, CIII), the harsh, rasping rhyme-sounds used throughout are the 'auditory correlative' of the exasperation and violence of frustrated passion. And, in the second place, Dante is not hampered by the difficulties of the form and—save in the so-called 'double *sestina*', *Amor, tu vedi ben* (*Rime*, CII)—rises to some of his most impressive heights. Let me exemplify this by quoting from the other member of the group, *Io son venuto al punto de la rota* (*Rime*, C). Here the difficulties are, strictly speaking, more thematic than formal. As in the *sestina* Dante is imitating Arnaut Daniel. This time he takes from the latter's *canso*, *Quan chai la fuelha*, what was in any case the well-worn theme of the 'lover in winter'. The gist of this is neatly summarized in two lines from a well-known medieval Latin poem:[1]

> Modo frigescit quicquid est,
> sed solus ego caleo.*

[1] *De ramis cadunt folia*, ll. 19–20, in *Oxford Book of Medieval Latin Verse*, ed. F. J. E. Raby (Oxford, 1959), p. 353.

* 'Now everything grows cold: but I alone am hot.'

The subject is then unmistakably 'littérature', and Dante goes out of his way to accentuate the 'unreality' of his theme by restating it five times in the five stanzas, giving a periphrasis for 'it is midwinter' in terms of five different sciences carefully arranged in descending order, respectively: astronomy, meteorology, zoology, botany, geology. Each variation is perfectly symmetrical, the contrast being introduced in the tenth line of each stanza, and in every case by the conjunction 'e' used adversatively. But the result is far from being a dull if well-made conceit. Dante goes from strength to strength until in the bleak winter landscape of the fifth stanza he gives us an almost perfect example of how to convey feelings through sounds and the evocation of things:

> Versan le vene le fummifere acque
> per li vapor che la terra ha nel ventre,
> che d'abisso li tira suso in alto;
> onde cammino al bel giorno mi piacque
> che ora è fatto rivo, e sarà mentre
> che durerà del verno il grande assalto;
>   la terra fa un suol che par di smalto,
> e l'acqua morta si converte in vetro
> per la freddura che di fuor la serra:
> e io de la mia guerra
> non son però tornato un passo a retro,
> né vo' tornar; ché se 'l martiro è dolce,
> la morte de' passare ogni altro dolce.*
>
>   (*Rime*, C, 53–65.)

* 'The springs spew forth fumy waters because the earth draws the gases that are in its bowels upwards from the abyss; so that a path that pleased me in fine weather is now a stream, and so will remain as long as winter's great onslaught endures; the earth has formed a crust like

Dante's Lyric Poetry

At this point we may as well concede that Dante is not a lyric poet in the nineteenth-century sense of the word. His poems are not the direct expression of his personality, nor the spontaneous overflow of emotion. They are too heterogeneous, the grip of the intellect and the delight in the art are too obvious. They scarcely satisfy any of the requirements of Romantic criticism, and where they seemed to do so—as in the sonnet, *Tanto gentile*, or the *canzone*, *Tre donne*—this was due in no small measure to misinterpretation from ignorance of the context. But rather than seek again to contest the validity or the sufficiency of those criteria, let us simply by-pass them completely. It will surely be agreed that a measure of extroversion, even theatricality, a love of construction, the ability to speak convincingly with many voices are not incompatible with artistic integrity and sincerity, and may all be highly desirable qualities in some forms of creative writing—in the drama for example. No one has seriously argued that *King Lear* is not great poetry because it has a plot, and because none of the characters speak alike. Since we have found some of these qualities in the poems we have examined, would it not perhaps be fruitful to approach Dante's poems somewhat as one would dramatic poetry? The answer is I think 'yes'—provided always that the implied comparison is not forced in any way. For what may be loosely described as the 'dramatic element' in Dante's poems determines many of the successes, and is

rock, and the dead waters turn into glass because of the cold that locks them in. And yet I have not withdrawn one step from the struggle, nor will I withdraw; for if suffering be sweet, death must be sweet above all things.'

also a kind of common denominator, a quality or tendency that unites poems of greatly differing date, style and matter, and one which links the lyric poetry as a whole with the *Comedy*, the work in which Dante's dramatic genius expressed itself in all its prodigious variety.

We may usefully begin a survey of the dramatic qualities in Dante's lyrics by presenting two other 'voices' from his mature period to complement the three quoted above. In the two *canzoni* from which they are taken Dante is fully 'engaged', speaking with the utmost seriousness on the subjects that touched him most deeply—justice and liberality. But his sincerity does not inhibit him from demonstrating his mastery of rhetoric, nor prevent him from achieving two quite distinct modes of expression: and in both he achieves poetry.

> Dimmi, che hai tu fatto,
> cieco avaro disfatto?
> Rispondimi, se puoi, altro che nulla.
> Maladetta tua culla,
> che lusingò cotanti sonni invano!
> Maladetto lo tuo perduto pane,
> che non si perde al cane!
> ché da sera e da mane
> hai raunato e stretto ad ambo mano
> ciò che sì tosto si rifà lontano.★
>
> (*Doglia mi reca, Rime*, CVI, 75–84.)

★ 'Tell me, what have you done, blind, undone miser? Answer me —if you can—other than "Nothing". Cursed be your cradle which beguiled so many dreams in vain; cursed be the bread you've wasted, that's not wasted on a dog; for evening and morning you have gathered and hoarded with both hands that which so quickly slips from your grasp again.'

E io, che ascolto nel parlar divino
consolarsi e dolersi
così alti dispersi,
l'essilio che m'è dato, onor mi tegno:
ché, se giudizio o forza di destino
vuol pur che il mondo versi
i bianchi fiori in persi,
cader co' buoni è pur di lode degno.★

(*Tre donne, Rime,* CIV, 73–80.)

That we are able to speak of Dante's voices at all is because so much of his poetry—like so much in the whole of medieval literature—is cast in the form of direct speech. And more often than not Dante is apparently addressing not us, the readers, but a specific person or group of people: a fellow poet, *madonna, donne, amanti*. 'Apparently', because the remarks were not usually meant to be confined exclusively to the named audience, any more than the *envois* are intended for the ears of the poems, or the *canzone, Voi che 'ntendendo il terzo ciel movete,* for the angels in the heaven of Venus. Dante was simply at ease when he had an audience to be addressed in the second person, and there is a compelling magic in many of the opening vocatives, as in:

O voi che per la via d'Amor passate.   (*Rime,* V.)

Donne ch'avete intelletto d'Amore.   (*Rime,* XIV.)

Deh peregrini che pensosi andate.   (*Rime,* XXXVI.)

Often, where his words are intended to produce a specific non-aesthetic effect on the audience, we have a

---

★ 'And I who listen to such noble exiles taking comfort and telling their grief in divine speech, I count as an honour the exile imposed on me: for if judgment or force of destiny does indeed desire that the world turn the white flowers into dark, it is still praiseworthy to fall with the good.'

proper, if fictitious, 'rhetorical situation'. Nor is it surprising in this respect that three of his *canzoni* (*Rime*, L, XC,
CII) are constructed according to the norms of the *ars
dictaminis* and are fully fledged *epistolae*, complete with
salutatio, *narratio* and a final *petitio* introduced by a resounding 'dunque' or 'però'. A rhetorical situation is already
a rudimentary dramatic situation, and only slight modi-
fications are necessary to convert a straightforward *epistola*
such as *La dispietata mente* (*Rime*, L) into the ingenious and
far more effective playlet of the only *ballata* to be included
in the *Vita Nuova* (*Rime*, IX; *VN*, XII).

Dante was not just following blind instinct in choosing
dramatic situations and accentuating their dramatic properties. He had a clear understanding of the immediacy
and therefore greater impact of direct speech. In the
fortieth chapter of the *Vita Nuova* he describes the genesis
of the well-known sonnet *Deh peregrini che pensosi andate*.
A thought struck him as he watched some pilgrims passing
along a street in Florence, and 'when they had passed out
of sight, I decided to write a sonnet in which I would
declare that unspoken thought: and, *so that it might excite
more compassion*, I decided to write as if I had spoken to
them'.* Even more striking in this respect is the pre-
history of two other sonnets in the *Vita Nuova* which
together form a complete little dramatic scene—not dis-
similar, incidentally, to the *Quem quaeritis* situation from
which the medieval religious drama developed. Here we

---

* 'Onde, passati costoro da la mia veduta, propuosi di fare uno
sonetto, ne lo quale io manifestasse ciò che io avea detto fra me mede-
simo; e acciò che più paresse pietoso, propuosi di dire come se io avesse
parlato a loro' (*VN*, XL, 5).

are able to compare the poems not only with the prose account (*VN*, xxii, esp. §§7–8) but also with what are obviously earlier attempts to shape the same material. In the first of these, *Onde venite voi così pensose?* (*Rime*, lxx), the whole sonnet is a monologue in which Dante anxiously questions a group of women about his lady. In the second, *Voi, donne, che pietoso atto mostrate* (*Rime*, lxxi), he introduces dialogue, limiting his question to the octet of the sonnet and then making one of the women reply. In the final version he allots a whole sonnet to his question, *Voi che portate la sembianza umile*, and a whole sonnet for the reply, *Se' tu colui c'hai trattato sovente* (*Rime*, xviii, xix; *VN*, xxii).

Casting our net a little wider now, we note that there are a number of poems which are semi-narrative in character, some of them being intensely dramatic in the common extended sense of the word, and many of them incorporating passages in direct speech. So we have the foreboding dream *A ciascun'alma presa* (*Rime*, i; *VN*, iii), a 'day'-dream, *Cavalcando l'altr'ier* (*Rime*, viii; *VN*, ix), an escapist vision, *Guido, i' vorrei* (*Rime*, lii), a hunting scene, *Sonar bracchetti* (*Rime*, lxi), the journey of a sigh up to heaven, *Oltre la spera* (*Rime*, xxxvii; *VN*, xli), an allegorical masque, *Tre donne* (*Rime*, civ), and in the *canzone*, *Donna pietosa* (*Rime*, xx; *VN*, xxiii), we have what is in effect a play within a play: Dante recounts how, during an illness, he cried out in delirium, how he was awakened by attendant women, and then how he related to *them* the terrifying apocalyptic dream that had led to the outcry. Even poems that are non-narrative in character may contain a short dramatized episode. Thus, in a poem of praise, *Donne ch'avete intelletto d'amore* (*Rime*, XIV; *VN*, XIX), Beatrice is made the subject of a 'court-scene', audaciously set in heaven. The angels and the souls of the blessed alike plead that Beatrice should be summoned from earth immediately in order to make heaven perfect. Pity alone speaks for the defence. God, as judge, acknowledges the justice of the plea but grants a stay of execution:

> Angelo clama in divino intelletto
> e dice: 'Sire, nel mondo si vede
> maraviglia ne l'atto che procede
> d'un'anima che 'nfin qua su risplende.'
> Lo cielo, che non have altro difetto
> che d'aver lei, al suo segnor la chiede,
> e ciascun santo ne grida merzede.
> Sola Pietà nostra parte difende,
>   che parla Dio, che di madonna intende:
> 'Diletti miei, or sofferite in pace
> che vostra spene sia quanto me piace
> là 'v'è alcun che perder lei s'attende,
> e che dirà ne lo inferno: O mal nati,
> io vidi la speranza de' beati.'*   (Lines 15–28.)

Or again, in a poem of abuse, when Dante wants to call his good friend Forese Donati a thief and a bastard, he does so

---

* 'An angel cries in the divine intellect, saying: "Lord, in the world there appears a marvel in act, proceeding from a soul whose splendour reaches even here on high!" Heaven, whose only lack is the lack of her, begs her from its Lord, and every saint cries out for this favour. Pity alone defends our cause, so that God, his mind on my lady, says: "My loved ones, bear it patiently that your hope remains as long as I please in the place where there is one who knows he will lose her, and who in hell will declare: O ill-fated ones, I have seen the hope of the blessed."'

indirectly and dramatically in two swift sketches: people shrink from Forese in the street and point him out as a common thief; his putative father lies anxiously awake for fear lest his 'son' should be caught red-handed.

> E già la gente si guarda da lui,
> chi ha borsa a lato, là dov'e' s'appressa,
> dicendo: 'Questi c'ha la faccia fessa
> è piuvico ladron negli atti sui.'
> E tal giace per lui nel letto tristo,
> per tema non sia preso a lo 'mbolare,
> che gli appartien quanto Giosepp' a Cristo.★
>
> (*Rime*, LXXVII, 5–11.)

So far we have dwelt on the more obvious and superficial manifestations of Dante's dramatic talent—his many voices, the frequency of direct speech, the poems and episodes that could as it were be enacted on stage or screen. But the heart and essence of that talent was Dante's constant tendency to translate ideas, qualities and emotions into concrete visible forms, and to set those forms in motion. He made spiritual events and actions apprehensible through the senses; this is what is meant when we say that he had the power of *representation*. And at this level almost all his poems are dramatic.

It was, for example, because he had that kind of gift that he was able—learning much from Guido Cavalcanti—to breathe new life into the most stereotyped, static and moribund parts of courtly love poetry. Typical poets of the

★ 'And already people who carry purses keep clear of him when he draws near, saying: "Scarface there is obviously a known thief."

And there's one who lies in bed distraught for fear that he'll be caught red-handed, who has as much to do with him as Joseph with Christ.'

The Mind of Dante

generation before Dante praised their ladies in terms such as these:

> Guardate lo vostro amoroso viso,
> l'angeliche bellezze
> e l'adornezze e la vostra bieltati.*¹

> Ov'è madonna e lo suo insegnamento,
> la sua bellezza e la gran canoscianza,
> lo dolze riso e lo bel parlamento,
> gli occhi e la bocca e la bella sembianza,
> e lo suo adornamento e cortesia?†²

Only exceptionally did Dante string together such weary, predominantly abstract technical terms to praise Beatrice. He tells us little about her at all, that little being either generic—'umile', 'onesta', 'gentile'—or emblematic—'color di perle ha quasi', 'vestita di nobilissimo colore'. For his innovation was to praise her as one praises God—through her *effects*.³ He does not tell us what she *was* but what she *did*: '...narrando alquanto de le sue vertudi effettive che de la sua anima procedeano' (*VN*, XIX, 18); '...parole ne le quali io dessi ad intendere de le sue mirabili ed eccellenti operazioni' (*VN*, XXVI, 4).‡ He does not even

---

¹ Mazzeo di Ricco, *Lo gran valore e lo presio amoroso*, ll. 24–6. Text from *Poeti del Duecento* (Milan–Naples, 1960), I, 153.

² Giacomino Pugliese, *Morte, perché m'hai fatta sì gran guerra*, ll. 31–5. Text *ibid*. p. 147.

³ This is made explicit in *Con*. III, viii, 15. The innovation is found in germ in a sonnet by Guinizzelli, *Io voglio del ver*, *Poeti del Duecento*, II, 472.

* 'Consider your face, so worthy of love, your angelic beauties, your graces and your loveliness.'

† 'Where is my lady and her perfect breeding, her beauty and great lore, her sweet smile and charming conversation, her eyes and lips, her lovely appearance, her graces and courtesy?'

‡ '...saying something about the outflowing goodness that emanated from her soul'; '...words in which I might express some of her miraculous and perfect doings [effects]'.

attempt to describe how she did what she did. We learn the quality of her 'action' only through its consequences, the reactions that it produced. But Dante's perfect expression of the emotions of trepidation, wonder and awe that she inspired in those who saw her passing along the street and greeting her acquaintance make her more radiantly and spiritually alive for us than a hundred qualitative epithets could have done.

> Tanto gentile e tanto onesta pare
> la donna mia quand'ella altrui saluta,
> ch'ogne lingua deven tremando muta,
> e li occhi no l'ardiscon di guardare.
> Ella si va, sentendosi laudare,
> benignamente d'umiltà vestuta;
> e par che sia una cosa venuta
> da cielo in terra a miracol mostrare.
>   Mostrasi sì piacente a chi la mira,
> che dà per li occhi una dolcezza al core,
> che 'ntender no la può chi no la prova:
> e par che de la sua labbia si mova
> un spirito soave pien d'amore,
> che va dicendo a l'anima: Sospira.*
>
>   (*Rime*, XXII; *VN*, XXVI.)

Praise of the lady is only one element in courtly love poetry. Another, possibly even more important, is the

---

* 'So gentle and so full of dignity my lady appears when she greets anyone that all tongues tremble and fall silent, and eyes dare not look at her. She goes on her way, hearing herself praised, graciously clothed with humility; and seems a thing come down from heaven to earth to make the miraculous known.

She appears so beautiful to those who gaze at her that through the eyes she sends a sweetness into the heart such as none can understand but he who experiences it: and from her lips seems to come a spirit, gentle and full of love, that says to the soul: "Sigh."'

description of the pangs of unrequited love. Italian poets before Dante normally expressed their sufferings in language like this:

> La mia vit'è sì fort'e dura e fera
> ch'eo non posso né viver né morire,
> anzi distruggo come al foco cera
> e sto com'on che non si pò sentire;* [1]

> E me e 'l meo in disamore ho, lasso,
> e amo solo lei che m'odia a morte;
> dolor più ch'altro forte
> e tormento crudele e angoscioso,
> e spiacer sì noioso
> che par mi strugga l'alma, il corpo e 'l core,
> sento sì, che 'l tinore
> propio non porea dir: perciò me 'n lasso.† [2]

Intensity was sought by accumulating nouns, verbs and adjectives of like import, spicing them with a little antithesis and topping them with one of some half-dozen prescribed similes ('storm', 'fire', 'ice', etc.). Dante's solution—and here he was most deeply indebted to Cavalcanti—was in effect to consider how such suffering was accounted for in the extremely elaborate medical and psychological science of the day, to simplify that descrip-

---

* 'My existence is so cruel, harsh and merciless that I can neither live nor die; I am consumed like wax before fire and am like a man out of his senses.'

[1] Guido delle Colonne, ll. 1–4. Text from *Poeti del Duecento*, I, 102.

† 'Alas!, I hold in disaffection myself and all things mine, and I love only her who hates me to the point of death. Grief more crushing than any other, a cruel and anguishing torment, a depression so intolerable that it seems to consume my soul, body and heart—all these I feel to such an extent that I could never express their true nature; and so I abandon the attempt.'

[2] Guittone d'Arezzo, *Ahi Deo, che dolorosa*, ll. 41–8. Text *ibid.* p. 193–4.

tion, and then to dramatize it. As a result the lover himself
is reduced to a mere stage. The actors in these poems are
his eyes, heart, mind, soul, blood, vital spirits, thoughts,
desires, sighs—all represented as independent agents, all
endowed with the faculty of speech. These are thrown into
turmoil and anarchy by the invading passion of love,
represented either by the lover's mental image of the lady
or by Love personified. When Dante describes how he saw
Beatrice for the first time and fell in love with her—or,
rather, knew that he would be dominated by love for
her—he offers us this little drama of the psyche, at once
scientific and poetic:

> quella virtù che ha più nobilitate,
> mirando nel piacere,
> s'accorse ben che 'l suo male era nato;
>   e conobbe 'l disio ch'era creato
> per lo mirare intento ch'ella fece;
> sì che piangendo disse a l'altre poi:
> 'Qui giugnerà, in vece
> d'una ch'io vidi, la bella figura,
> che già mi fa paura;
> che sarà donna sopra tutte noi,
> tosto che fia piacer de li occhi suoi'.*
>
>   (*E' m'incresce di me, Rime*, LXVII, 74–84.)

As with all lovers before him, his suffering brings him to
the point of death—but not a mention of the word 'morire'
in Dante's exact representation of the moment:

* ' . . . that faculty which is noblest [the mind], gazing into the beauty,
saw that its own suffering was born, and recognized the desire that was
caused by its own intense gazing; so that then it said weeping to the other
faculties: "Here, representing one whom I have seen, will come as soon
as it pleases her eyes, the beautiful image which already affects me with
fear and which will rule as mistress over us all." '

Ristretta s'è [l'anima] entro il mezzo del core
con quella vita che rimane spenta
solo in quel punto ch'ella si va via;
e ivi si lamenta
d'Amor, che fuor d'esto mondo la caccia;
e spessamente abbraccia
li spiriti che piangon tuttavia,
però che perdon la lor compagnia.* (*Ibid.* 35–42.)

This technique could be freely adapted to express other
and often complex mental processes or states of mind.
While on a journey he tries to cheer himself up by thinking
about his lady (*Deh ragioniamo, Rime,* LX); he is torn by
doubts about the nature of love (*Tutti li miei penser, Rime,*
X; *VN,* XIII), or, later, he finds it hard to reconcile the
claims of virtue and beauty (*Due donne, Rime,* LXXXVI); he
has a premonition that Beatrice is approaching (*Io mi senti'
svegliar, Rime,* XXI; *VN,* XXIV), or that she is going to die
(*Un dì si venne a me Malinconia, Rime,* LXXII). He remem-
bers Beatrice on the first anniversary of her death (*Era
venuta ne la mente mia, Rime,* XXX; *VN,* XXXIV). And then,
profoundly interesting and original, he experiences a
mental struggle between his desire to remain faithful to the
dead Beatrice and a new love for a 'gentile donna'. This
is expressed in four sonnets (*Rime,* XXXI–XXXIV; *VN,*
XXXV–XXXVIII), which trace the growth of this new inclination, and finally in the *canzone, Voi che 'ntendendo*

* 'The soul has shrunk back into the innermost heart with such life as
is extinguished only at the instant of her departure; and there she com-
plains against Love who is driving her out of this world; and embraces
again and again the vital spirits who mourn continually the loss of their
companion.'

(*Rime*, LXXIX; *Con.* II), which brilliantly dramatizes the moment of surrender to the 'donna gentile'.

This same *canzone* illustrates particularly clearly what we may regard as the last of Dante's 'dramatic gifts': his concern for solid, formal construction. The first stanza is a formal *proemio*, addressed to the angels in the heaven of Venus, at the close of which (lines 10–13) Dante states what are to be the themes of the following stanzas: 'Io vi dirò del cor la novitate' (developed in the second stanza), 'come l'anima trista piange in lui' (the theme of stanza 3), 'e come un spirto contra lei favella, che vien pe' raggi de la vostra stella'* (the theme of stanza 4). The poem is completed by a *congedo* or *envoi*, which, as nearly always in Dante, is an integral part of the poem: here it seems to give a veiled warning that the poem should be read allegorically, that is, in the way it was to be expounded by Dante in the *Convivio*. Many other *canzoni* share this same logical, clearly articulated structure, in which one theme is developed in three, four or five stages—each occupying one stanza—to reach a conclusion or climax in the last stanza; and in which this, the body of the poem, is framed by the highly relevant *proemio* and *congedo*. And even where this particular pattern is not followed, the structure is invariably clear and intellectually satisfying. Now, if it was Dante's concern for *dispositio* that set his *canzoni* apart from those of his Provençal and Italian predecessors, it was his interest in the long poem, the *canzone*, that distinguished his

---

* 'I will tell you of my heart's strange condition—how my sad soul weeps in it, and how a spirit disputes with her, who comes in the rays from your star.'

work from that of Cavalcanti, which did so much to determine Dante's development in the first decade of his career. Dante clearly felt the need to treat his themes exhaustively. Thus, apart from the evidence of his many *canzoni*, one notices that a number of poems fall into groups and require to be read as such. There are, for example, the early sonnets examining his condition, included in *VN*, XIII–XVI. Then there is the short cycle for the 'gentile donna'; later the four *canzoni petrose*, and the uncompleted scheme to compose fourteen *canzoni* and expound them in the *Convivio*. It was this same driving need to express himself fully that led him to write an extended work like the *Vita Nuova*. And it is in the construction of this *libellum* that I find its greatest artistic merit, the property which finally makes it one, successful work of art, and Dante's greatest poem before the *Comedy*.

To advance such a claim for any one aspect of this amazingly rich little book is obviously invidious, and it certainly requires qualification and justification. It is perhaps possible only in the context of this essay, where I have chosen to discuss the poems that Dante included in the *Vita Nuova* on the same terms as the others, and also to consider the *Vita Nuova* not just together with his poems but as itself a work of poetry. To do this, one has to ignore something like half the prose, that is, all those largely pedestrian passages in which Dante describes the actual composition of his poems, divides and glosses them, or makes brief excursions into literary and linguistic theory, astronomy and numerology. And when both poems and expository prose are thus left out of the account, it follows necessarily that one ignores a dimension of the work that Dante was at great pains to establish: its objectivity, its 'authority' in the medieval sense of the word, its status as a *book*. As Dante presents the matter, we are to believe that his role was limited to that of copyist and commentator. The poems are 'given' and are merely transcribed; the narrative passages are selected and copied from the book of his memory; his original contributions are the divisions and glosses.

However, there are occasions when a narrow and one-sided view of a work of art can serve a useful purpose. And nothing obliges us to accept Dante's presentation of the book at its face value. The poems were indeed all written beforehand,[1] and this is all the more reason for reading each one independently and judging each on its own merits. The professedly 'original' expository prose has no aesthetic value. It is in the narrative or descriptive prose —utterly unlike a transcript from a diary—that the essence of the book is to be sought: in the new ideas it introduces, in the story it tells, and in the way that story is told.

All three elements in the narrative prose are vitally important. There can be no doubt whatever that the *Vita Nuova* would be poorer, and poorer as literature, if the 'intelletto d'amore' evident in the prose were not fuller and deeper than that evident, or even implicit, in the poems. By the time he wrote the *Vita Nuova* Dante's understanding of love had been enriched by his reading in works that lay outside the courtly tradition. In his brilliant and now fundamental book on the *Vita Nuova*,[2] Domenico de

[1] Some doubts attach to the *canzone, Donna pietosa, VN,* XXIII.
[2] *Il libro della 'Vita Nuova'* (Florence, 1961).

Robertis gathers many striking parallels, some well known, others hitherto unnoticed, from Cicero's *De amicitia* (*Laelius*) and its Christian descendant, the *De Spirituali Amicitia* of Aelredus, from the Bible and in particular the Psalms, and from works by St Augustine, St Bernard, Hugh and Richard of St Victor. He shows, to put it very briefly, that Dante appropriated virtually all the characteristics attributed by Christian writers to *amor Dei*—from love as self-sufficient and disinterested, as a source of beatitude, humility and love for all men, to the fundamental one of spiritual rebirth, *renovatio*, *vita nova* brought about by that love. He took them and used them to interpret, glorify and consecrate his love for Beatrice. Without these new concepts the *Vita Nuova* simply could not have existed. But, at the same time, their presence in itself would do nothing to make the *Vita Nuova* a work of art. What matters in this respect is that Dante assimilated them, lived them, made them part of himself, and was thus able to express them in a poetic narrative which has nothing of the philosophical dialogue, the tractate or the sermon.

We have now limited our field of inquiry to the purely artistic merits of the narrative prose element in the *Vita Nuova*. For the sake of simplicity let us assume that these merits may be grouped under two heads: first, the quality of the prose, considered sentence by sentence, paragraph by paragraph; secondly, the construction of the story as a whole. There is unfortunately no space to demonstrate the quality of the prose here. But, in a sense, there is no need to, for in essence the prose shares the characteristics, virtues and limitations of the best poems included in the *Vita Nuova*. At the stylistic level, it has the same limited, abstract, elevated vocabulary; it avoids the same *ornatus*; the syntax is not that of colloquial speech but is simple nevertheless. As in the verse, the most important expressive element is the rhythm and music of the language. There are the same dramatic qualities: each episode is a scene; dialogue is more frequent than ever; Love is personified; the condition of the lover's soul is represented just as in the verse, so are the beatific effects of Beatrice on all who see her. The prose is more consistent than the verse. Being free of the exigencies of metre, rhyme and strophe, it is often richer and fuller. It offers tantalizing glimpses of particular events, real Florentine customs. But notwithstanding the clear distinction between the language of poetry and that of prose explicitly made by Dante in the work itself (*VN*, xxv), the narrative prose is a vehicle comparable in all respects to the verse. Similarly, the truth it offers is not essentially different from that of the poems, and bears the same remote relationship to what we call 'real' events in Dante's life—a fact so often overlooked in the past.

As with the 'intelletto d'amore', so with the prose: had it not been as appropriate and expressive as the following typical paragraph, the *Vita Nuova* would exist simply as an anthology of poems:

Ora, tornando al proposito, dico che poi che la mia beatitudine mi fue negata, mi giunse tanto dolore, che, partito me da le genti, in solinga parte andai a bagnare la terra d'amarissime lagrime. E poi che alquanto mi fue sollenato questo lagrimare, misimi ne la mia camera, là ov'io potea lamentarmi sanza essere udito; e quivi, chiamando misericordia a la donna de la cortesia, e dicendo 'Amore, aiuta lo tuo fedele', m'addormentai come un pargoletto battuto lagrimando.* (XII, 12.)

Nevertheless, given the experience and understanding, given their artistic expression, I repeat that what ultimately makes the *Vita Nuova* a successful and completely original work of art is its construction. For what might have been just a series of episodes are ordered and fused into a unified narrative with beginning, middle and end. We have not just a love story, but a story of the progressive discovery of love; not just the story of a *vita*, but of a *vita nova*, a spiritual rebirth through love.

There is of course much conscious art in the construction of the book. One thinks immediately of the constant association with Beatrice of the number nine, and the long-delayed explanation (XXIX) of its significance—that it meant that she was a miracle, nine being the product of the perfect number multiplied by itself, a trinity of trinities. One thinks of the symmetrical arrangement of the poems, whereby twenty-eight shorter poems are grouped around a trinity of long *canzoni* to create the scheme: 10 + I + 4 + I + 4 + I + 10. Or of the anticipations of Beatrice's death—in dreams of that event (III, XXIII), in the death of her companion (VIII) and then of her father (XXII). Or of

---

* 'Now, returning to my theme, I say that when my beatitude was denied me, such grief came upon me that, withdrawing from all company, I went to a lonely spot to bathe the ground with the bitterest of tears. And when my weeping had eased a little, I went to my room where I could lament without being heard. And there, calling for pity to the lady of courtesy and saying "Love, help your servant", I fell asleep still sobbing like a child after a beating.'

the *coup de théâtre* with which the news of Beatrice's death is announced: a *canzone* left unfinished, a verse from Jeremiah's Lamentations introduced without any preparation. But although one can see from the *Comedy* that Dante attached great importance to numerology, symmetry, formal correspondences and suspense in the composition of long works, it is not in these accidents that his constructive genius is to be found. That genius shows first in that the principal episodes are made stages along the road to the full discovery of love; and, secondly, in that these episodes are not just so many beads on one string but fall into a pattern, in which the same cycle of events is twice enacted—once at a purely human, physical level, and then at a religious or metaphysical level.

In the early chapters Dante is presented as the courtly lover in the final stage of evolution, that is, 'serving' joyfully in the expectation of 'reward', that reward now being attenuated to mere recognition by the lady. The first crisis occurs when that recognition is denied, and it is followed by a period of unhappiness, of selfish lamentation at Beatrice's indifference to, or even mockery of, his love. This phase ends with the first major 'discovery' about love: that true love should issue in disinterested praise of the beloved and is its own reward, a joy that can never fail. With the consequent resolve to praise Beatrice, the first cycle is complete. The second again opens with a period of equilibrium and joy, but this is swiftly shattered by the second crisis. Like the first, this is caused from without, but is of an altogether different order. Beatrice herself is taken from him by death. Once again Dante's love survives the blow, but only to be a source of tribulation. His joy *has* failed. He is as inconsolable for her loss as he had been for the loss of her greeting. Because his love brings him only sorrow, it is not true love, and is thus seriously threatened by the living attractions of the 'gentile donna'. This second period of lamentation ends with a vision of Beatrice in heaven and the final 'discovery' about love: that the death of the beloved should cause only transient grief; that true love should not only survive death but become a source of greater joy, now that the beloved has become pure spirit and has increased in both beauty and virtue. Again Dante resolves to praise Beatrice and, ultimately, to say of her what had never before been said of a woman. The first cycle ended with the *canzone*, *Donne ch'avete*, the second with the *Vita Nuova* itself—already unprecedented praise for a woman! Paradise is twice lost from external causes, and twice regained through a deeper understanding of love coming from within.

We know that this solution, too, was premature and short-lived. The term of desire was still Beatrice and not God. The work was still a poem of 'courtly love', ignoring everything outside that ideal love, indifferent to reality, innocent of morality. In the *Comedy* Dante is seen to need not consolation but redemption. Nevertheless, it is this work, in its attempt to present his own experience in a poetic and universalized form, in its insistence on love, in the beauty and rightness of its language, in the deeply satisfying construction of the whole, which is the most significant and worthy precursor of the *Comedy*, and Dante's greatest achievement as a lyric poet.

5

DANTE'S POLITICAL THOUGHT

U. LIMENTANI

It has been maintained that each century has found in Dante's political thought what it wished to find; it is more true to say (or so it seems to a prejudiced reader like myself) that most writers have sought in Dante's works a confirmation of their preconceived ideas about his political views. Medieval historians, literary critics, theologians, students of medieval philosophy, of history of the law and of political thought have all scanned his works from their own viewpoints, and come to diametrically opposite conclusions. Some considered that Dante's proposals were strikingly original, even revolutionary; others that he repeated well-worn theories. Some suggested that he was an extremist in his Ghibellinism; others that he was a moderate writer. Some believed that his profound knowledge of the law affected his political thought; others that his equipment in this field was quite superficial. Confusion is made worse by the fact that, in order to make up one's mind about Dante's political thought as a whole, one has to have views about the chronology of his writings: a subject that is, to say the least, controversial.

When, therefore, I say that it is my intention to give a general account of Dante's political ideas, letting Dante speak for himself, and disregarding whenever possible

113

what others (and how many others!) have said about him, I must add in the same breath that this praiseworthy intention will only too frequently have to be qualified, because at a great number of points a choice between two or more interpretations will be inevitable, and this choice will have to be personal, or will have to endorse or reject what others have written.

To plunge deep into troubled waters from the beginning, one has to decide whether Dante's various political writings show any evidence of a marked change, even, as some critics have suggested, of a conversion at some point or other. For Dante expressed political views in the *Convivio*, which can be dated fairly securely to a few years before the election of Henry VII in 1308, in the epistles which he wrote during Henry's campaigns in Italy (1310–13), in the *Monarchia*, and in the *Comedy*; and a span of not much less than fifteen years must have separated the *Convivio* from the completion of the *Comedy*. Definite stages in the process of the gradual formation of Dante's political thought have been traced by various writers. That a change of outlook—the one and decisive change of outlook from the days of his youth in Florence—had taken place at a fairly early stage, and certainly before he wrote the *Convivio*, is hinted at by Dante himself when he recalls in the *Monarchia* (II, i, 2) that he once thought that the Romans had conquered the world by force of arms alone, without any foundation of right: a characteristically Guelf view, which, he tells us, he later rejected. Apart from this, it is undeniable that a man whose habits of mind leaned towards meditation should ponder upon problems, clear up certain aspects of them, put them into focus, and work out details; and that, as he wrote, he should give us from time to time the results of his meditations and readings and of his reactions to historical events. But the tendency to detect one or more *volte-faces* in the evolution of Dante's thought has been overdone. Lack of consistency, or views expressed without adequate reflexion, should not be assumed too lightly in the case of Dante. That he did not change his mind, or discover by degrees his real and final outlook on politics, is the belief that underlies the following observations.

A preoccupation with politics was ever-present in Dante's mind. It was politics that determined the course of his life, and, down to the *Paradiso*, there is hardly one of the works written after his exile in which politics are absent for long. While still a young man, he was drawn into active participation in the political affairs of Florence. In accordance with the prevalent tradition of his native city, and indeed with the long-standing allegiance of his family, he was a typical Florentine Guelf: ready to support the Pope, but up in arms against him if he tried to encroach upon the interests of Florence. At the end of 1301 Dante had to leave his city never to return to it, exiled as a White Guelf, when the Black Guelfs gained power with the help of Pope Boniface VIII. After supporting the joint attempts of his fellow exiles, both White Guelfs and Ghibellines, to oust the usurpers from Florence, he became disgusted with the futility of his companions, and left their ranks to spend the rest of his life in isolation. For this fact we have the evidence of Dante's own words, when he makes his ancestor

Cacciaguida say to him in the *Paradiso* (xvii, 68–9): 'sì ch'a te fia bello Averti fatta parte per te stesso.'*

Did Dante remain a Guelf for the rest of his life? Or did he become a Ghibelline, as his support for the Emperor Henry VII has led most people to believe? In canto x of the *Inferno* he represents himself as not having consciously abjured his Guelf faith, for here he proudly and clearly contrasts his political allegiance with that of the Ghibelline leader Farinata. Of course, this cannot be taken as a statement of his beliefs at the time of writing, as one must distinguish between Dante the author and Dante the character in the *Comedy*.

But at this point the problem, whether Guelf or Ghibelline, seems to become unimportant, bound up as it is with the narrow sphere of municipal politics; for the experience of exile, and the lesson of many events that had shaken not only his world but the wider world of Christendom, had led Dante to enter a new dimension in politics. From now on his preoccupation will no longer be, or rather will not primarily be, the welfare of Florence, but the welfare of mankind. He had seen the effects of civil strife, of wars between cities, of the struggle between the Pope and the King of France. He had read the many pronouncements that this struggle had evoked from the Pope (particularly the bull *Unam Sanctam* which made a deep impression upon him) and from Philippe le Bel's propagandists. His wanderings had widened his horizon, and forced upon him the consideration of a universal problem. Given to specu-

---

* 'So that it will be well for thee to have made thee a party for thyself.'

lation as he was, he saw that his task was not so much to be active in practical affairs as to discover ideal conditions for the happiness of humanity, to expound his system and, by proving its truth, to persuade men to adopt it.

It was in these early years of his exile that his political thought took shape, and I do not think that he ever had cause to modify it in its essentials. Its first enunciation is in a digression: two chapters (chapters IV–V) in the fourth book of the *Convivio*. Its full exposition is to be found in the *Monarchia*, a treatise in three books, which follows the syllogistic method of the scholastics.

The world, as Dante had been forcibly brought to realize, is torn by discord. Greed for material things ('cupiditas') is the main fault, greed which is allowed to dictate the actions of men. Only a cessation of strife, the establishment of universal peace, can ensure the happiness of mankind and allow men to pursue the ultimate aim for which God has destined them on earth, that of exercising constantly and to the full their distinctive quality, the 'virtus intellectiva' (*Mon.* I, iii, 7). Indeed, 'peace' is the *leitmotif* that runs through the whole of the first book of the *Monarchia*, an intense longing for peace and justice, which could only be achieved if the world were ruled by a single monarch—the Emperor. This is the proposition that Dante sets out to prove in the first book of his treatise: the necessity for the happiness of mankind of an Emperor who is free from greed, since his jurisdiction has no boundaries, who can therefore desire nothing and can be wholly just in his rule (*Mon.* I, xi, 12). The assumption that underlies this proposition is that mankind is not merely the sum total of a large number of men but an entity which can be considered *per se* (*Mon.* i, ii, 8); this far-reaching and far-sighted notion of a universal human society, a notion greatly in advance of his times, provides a framework for the close reasoning of the first book and, one might add, postulates the requirement of a universal monarch to guide humanity.

Dante sketches only in the barest outline the details of how the Emperor is to exercise his functions; the sovereignty of the various communes, principalities and kingdoms is not disputed, but they are to be subject to the higher sovereignty of the Emperor, who must be held to be 'minister omnium' (*Mon.* i, xii, 12), the legislator, judge and ruler who keeps kingdoms, principalities and republics on the right path, who ministers to the welfare of all his subjects, and safeguards justice and freedom for everybody. The Emperor's rule is not understood in the sense that he should solve every petty problem or municipal difficulty, but that he should supply individual princes and republics with the 'principia universalia' (*Mon.* i, xiv, 8), so that they in their turn may prescribe the laws they deem proper. Only in doubtful cases will the Emperor intervene to make a decision or to right wrongs. Owing to the moral and intellectual superiority imparted by his position of pre-eminence, the Emperor is the only one who can interpret and master the principles of the natural law from which ordinary laws derive, and which are hidden by passions and appetites from less exalted men.

What is the place of Italy, one may inquire at this point, within the wider context of the Empire? The question arises from a view that was fashionable during the last century: Dante was thought to have foreshadowed the national unity of Italy and, as some writers have more recently maintained, to have assumed the existence of a kingdom of Italy, with the Emperor as its sovereign, in other words, the existence of another political institution interposed between the Empire and the various republics and principalities. A dispassionate examination of Dante's works shows that this view is unfounded. It is true that Dante's wanderings during his exile had the result of widening his experience and his interests from municipal to Italian horizons. He became more aware of the fact that Italy formed a cultural and linguistic unit. Indeed, the fortunes of Italy were ever present to his mind. Even when he was concentrating on the problem of the Empire, the plight of Italy was the thought that remained uppermost: thus, for instance, Henry, in the thirtieth canto of the *Paradiso* (137–8), is described as one 'ch'a drizzare Italia Verrà';* and in the invective of the sixth canto of the *Purgatorio* the focus is on Italy, and the supreme problem of the vacancy of the Empire is seen primarily as one that affects Italy.

But all this does not warrant the conclusion that Dante thought in terms of Italy as a political unit. In the whole of the *Monarchia* there are to be found but two passing references to Italy (*Mon.* II, iii, 16; II, xii, 8), and it is clear that his political aspirations in regard to Italy do not go beyond the preservation of local and regional autonomies under the supervision of imperial representatives, and a fruitful collaboration between the imperial government and the

---

* 'Who will come to set Italy straight.'

republics and rulers of Italy; in other words, they do not go beyond what Henry had proposed to achieve.[1] For Dante was well acquainted with the realities of the political situation of Italy and never showed any sign of ignoring them. Did he not address the epistle written on the occasion of the coming of Henry VII not only to Italy's kings and to the Roman senators, but also 'Ducibus Marchionibus Comitibus atque Populis' (*Ep*. v, 1)? Therefore, when one tries to define Dante's thought about Italy's place within the Empire, one can go no further than saying that this country was destined to occupy a special position only because the imperial authority had its source within its boundaries or, more precisely, in Rome.

The mention of Rome brings us to the second part in Dante's chain of argument. The Emperor was, of course, the Roman Emperor, in direct line of succession to the emperors of ancient Rome. That he was in fact a German emperor did not affect the issue in the eyes of Dante or of many of his contemporaries; the holder of the Empire was axiomatically the 'Romanus Princeps', so strongly had the idea of the supremacy of Rome survived through the centuries. Dante accepts this idea wholeheartedly, and indeed makes it a vital part of his system. He devotes to it the second book of the *Monarchia*, whose subject is that the Roman people took up the office of the universal monarchy by right (*Mon*. II, ii, 1): proving this proposition meant proving that the Roman Emperor is the monarch whom, as demonstrated in the first book, mankind clearly

[1] See G. Vinay's edition of the *Monarchia* (Florence, Sansoni, 1950), pp. 188–9, n. 15.

needs. The triumphal progress of that 'popolo santo' (*Con.*
IV, iv, 10) is now rehearsed from ordeal to ordeal, from
victory to victory, to make it abundantly clear that they
were a heroic and extraordinary people appointed by God
to fulfil a necessary role in his harmonious design, endowed
by him for this purpose with nobility, piety, righteousness,
the spirit of justice and military valour, and predestined to
universal domination, as attested by many visible signs—
the innumerable prodigies recorded in their annals. Like-
wise, the interpretation of Roman history as a 'certamen',
a competition or a duel, which may induce some readers
of the *Monarchia* to raise their eyebrows, is intended to
drive home the point that Rome achieved greatness because God had decreed that she should, since in a duel
God's will is manifested in favour of the winner. It is fair
to add that Dante accepted the duel as a sign of God's
judgement only with some important qualifications: a
duel should be entered as an *ultima ratio* and, above all,
when the fighters or duellers go into the fray moved by
'zelum iustitie' (*Mon.* II, ix, 4). Only in this way is resorting to a duel (or to war) resorting to God's judgement.
Dante then conceived history as a manifestation of the will
of God, and took the portion of history which seemed to
be the most significant of all (that of the Roman people in
their progress towards acquiring sovereignty over all men
at the time of the Empire) as evidence of the way which has
been prescribed for the return of justice and peace upon
earth. The Roman people are seen as an instrument of the
design of Providence, and the glorious pagan past, which
was decreed and predestined, is projected through the

lamentable contemporary state of affairs on to a future which is shown, by a correct reading of history, to be in accordance with the will of God. Fittingly, in this account of history viewed as a great contest in which the nations fought under the watchful eye of their Creator, poets and saints as well as historians are taken to be equally trustworthy sources;[1] Dante quotes Livy, Virgil, St Luke, Boethius in the same breath, but Virgil is the source *par excellence*. The *Aeneid* of Virgil was deemed to be as historically accurate as it was poetic. It was the proof of the continuity of the nation. Virgil, the celebrator of the Roman Empire, is as much Dante's guide in the *Monarchia* as Virgil, the poet and the symbol, is his guide in the *Comedy*.

The two propositions expounded and proved true in the first and second book of the *Monarchia*, namely that an Emperor is necessary for the happiness of mankind, and that the imperial dignity belongs *de iure* to the Roman people, are the indispensable premisses to the third book, in which Dante tackles what seemed to him the central problem of his time and of all times. Given (as he had proved) that a monarch is necessary for the welfare of men, and that this universal monarch is, according to God's will, the Roman Emperor, how did it happen that for a long time the design of Providence had been thwarted? Two causes seem to have been uppermost in Dante's mind as having been responsible for the decadence of the universal monarchy: the absence from Italy of the German Emperors (that is to say their neglect of their duties, for, instead of

[1] See Vinay, *op. cit.* p. 165, n. 18.

wisely and justly ruling the world from Rome, they had preferred to devote their attention to their German domains); and the confusion of the ecclesiastical power and the civil power.

It is mainly with this latter problem that the third book of the *Monarchia* is concerned. It seeks to establish the separation of the temporal power from the spiritual power, and to prove that the authority of the Roman monarch, who is by right the monarch of the world, derives immediately from God, and not from the Vicar of God (*Mon.* III, i, 5): a secular, or anti-hierocratical solution to the problem of the happiness of men on earth, and therefore a proposition which undermined the very basis of the claims to supremacy which had been repeatedly put forward by the Popes, which Boniface VIII had forcefully asserted in the bull *Unam Sanctam*, and of which Clement V had often taken care to remind Henry VII. Indeed, more than one of the arguments based on the Scriptures, on history, and on reason, which Dante proceeds to refute, such as 'quod-cumque ligaveris' and the 'Two Swords' (*Mon.* III, viii and ix), had been used by Boniface. One of the refuted arguments based on history deserves a special mention: it was founded on the Donation of Constantine which, it was held, created a relationship of dependence of one of the two supreme authorities on the other, since Constantine was alleged to have donated the capital of the Empire, Rome, 'cum multis aliis Imperii dignitatibus' (*Mon.* III, x, 1) to the Pope; the latter thereby enjoyed prerogatives which had their most conspicuous recognition in the coronation of the Emperor by the Pope. Dante, who does not deny the Donation as a historical fact, holds that it was illegal, for Constantine could not alienate his imperial rights, as this would have been contrary to the nature of his office, and would have amounted to a destruction of the Empire. On the other hand, the Church could not receive temporal possessions because of the express prohibition in Matthew's Gospel. The Church can receive temporal possessions, not become the owner of them, only to administer their income for its own upkeep and for the poor. The Donation of Constantine, which in the *Comedy* is repeatedly blamed for being the origin of the avarice and corruption of the Church, is seen in the *Monarchia* as a principal cause of the confusion of the two powers and of the decline of the authority of the Empire. But in both works it is damned with equal vehemence as 'la cagion che il mondo ha fatto reo'* (*Purg.* XVI, 104).

The concluding chapter of the treatise (*Mon.* III, xvi) sets the seal on the arguments meant to prove the direct derivation from God of the power of the Emperor. Man has two aims: happiness on earth, and happiness in the eternal life. The first is achieved through philosophy, by means of the moral and intellectual virtues (the cardinal virtues); the second, through revealed truths, by means of the theological virtues. Since man is apt to forget aims and means on account of cupidity, unless he is held in check, two guides are necessary: the Pope to guide mankind to eternal life, in accordance with revealed truth, and the Emperor, to guide mankind to temporal happiness in accordance with the teachings of philosophy. This latter purpose

---

* 'The cause that has made the world iniquitous.'

could hardly be achieved, unless mankind, having first brought under control the stormy allurements of cupidity, found freedom and peace. To this goal the Roman Prince should strive with all his strength. Since the disposition of this world is in a direct relationship with the disposition of the rotating Heavens, it is necessary that the protector of the world be established by him who has a direct and immediate vision of this disposition, by him who pre-ordained it. God then elects the Emperor, and the electors can only be considered as revealers of God's providential will. By this, and by the several arguments that precede it, it is proved that the temporal monarch receives his authority from the source of all authority, and not from the Pope.

At the end of the chapter, a final paragraph puts in its proper light Dante's thought about the relationship be-tween the two powers. The solution of the problem, whether the monarch's authority depends directly upon God or upon others, should not, he says (*Mon.* III, xvi, 17–18), be taken so literally as to exclude absolutely the Roman Prince being in some kind of relationship of sub-jection ('in aliquo...non subiaceat') to the Pope, because this mortal happiness of ours is in a certain way ('quodam modo') ordered towards eternal happiness. Let, therefore, Caesar observe towards Peter that reverence which a first-born owes to his father, so that, illumined by the light of paternal grace, he may more effectively irradiate the world, the charge of which has been given to him by God.

This last passage has been taken by many to nullify and flagrantly contradict the spirit and the letter of the rest of the book, and to destroy at one stroke that independence of the two powers which Dante had been at such pains to demonstrate. It has recently been described as a striking and sudden change of attitude, a *volte-face* which 'suggests a complete breakdown of Dante's dualism'.[1] Others have tended to minimize the importance of the passage, by passing it off as a 'last-minute correction' by which 'nothing is really changed'[2]; or as an addition of one who, re-reading his book, realizes that he has made a mistake or has at least overstepped the mark, and hastily tries to find an excuse.[3]

Yet it would be uncharacteristic of Dante to act in this way; for where else does he patch up his work in a hurry, or have to retrace his steps through having inadequately thought out a problem? It is important to bear in mind that the independence of the temporal power, far from being denied, is reaffirmed in the very last words of the treatise, where, as Gilson pointed out,[4] one and the same sentence declares that Caesar owes reverence to Peter, and that Caesar has been given charge of the world directly by God. And, again, it may be observed that the reverence owed by the Emperor to the Pope is not introduced at the last minute but had been previously implied, particularly in the chapter (*Mon.* III, iv, 20) in which Dante deals with the two 'magna luminaria' of Genesis, the sun and the moon, the Pope and the Emperor. As for the seeming

[1] M. Wilks, *The problem of sovereignty in the later Middle Ages* (Cambridge University Press, 1963), p. 145.

[2] A. P. d'Entrèves, *Dante as a political thinker* (Oxford, 1952), p. 58.

[3] B. Nardi, *Saggi di filosofia dantesca* (Milano–Genova–Roma–Napoli, Soc. Anon. Ed. Dante Alighieri, 1930), p. 285.

[4] E. Gilson, *Dante et la philosophie* (Paris, Librairie Philosophique J. Vrin, 2e éd., 1953), p. 186.

contradiction between the complete autonomy of the Emperor proclaimed so steadfastly as the main contention of the treatise, and the (albeit qualified) subjection to the Pope that turns up in the last paragraph, an explanation can be suggested. In a recent work,[1] which it is impossible to summarize here because of its inevitable complexity, Gustavo Vinay stresses that in Dante's mind the Averroistic view of a clear-cut distinction between the earthly and the heavenly sphere (and, therefore, of the autonomy of earthly life and earthly happiness) co-existed with the knowledge that there is a continuity between life on earth and life in Heaven. Dante felt very strongly the need of being certain that life on earth has a meaning and a purpose of its own, and expressed this feeling, as was customary with him, by means of sharply defined categories. He was convinced even then, however, that the man who can achieve perfect happiness on earth through the pursuit of knowledge is that very same Christian who hopes for happiness in another life; he was convinced that only in the next life are our problems solved, although he could discuss the problem of happiness on earth without taking this particular consideration into account until the end of the book, and without thereby vitiating his argument. In other words, when he qualified what he had written before, he did not recant or in any way renounce his belief in the autonomy of the earthly life, but he conceded that the hope of another happiness may intensify an already relatively perfect earthly happiness. Thus earthly happiness can be seen to

[1] G. Vinay, *Interpretazione della 'Monarchia' di Dante* (Florence, F. Le Monnier, 1962).

be intrinsically ordered towards celestial happiness, but only 'quodam modo' (for being happy or unhappy on earth does not necessarily imply happiness or unhappiness in Heaven), and Caesar can be seen to owe reverence to Peter, not because he should receive orders or even advice in temporal matters, but because the Church is the guide to celestial happiness, and the Emperor will more effectively irradiate the world (that is, secure peace) if he is not only illumined by the grace of God but also blessed by the Pontiff.

Another, and more momentous, alleged *volte-face* in Dante's political ideas has been detected by those critics who hold that when he came to write the *Comedy* he repudiated the views expounded in the *Monarchia*: 'a tremendous change in Dante's whole outlook', as one writer put it.[1] In the *Comedy*, it is pointed out, the traditional relationship of subordination of reason to faith is re-established, and thus the philosophical justification of the independence of the Empire from the Church, namely the parallel and separate 'duo fines' to which man is preconstituted and the two guides that are necessary thereto, goes overboard. Some critics[2] have even gone so far as to see in the *Monarchia* a foreboding of the spirit of the Renaissance, and in the *Comedy* a retrogression to a medieval outlook. Such an opinion presupposes that the *Monarchia* represents an earlier stage of Dante's political thought, and that the *Comedy* was conceived and written after the *Monarchia*. This would be neat and convenient for interpreters, who could compare the various periods of the poet's work without troublesome overlaps. It is my inten-

[1] A. P. d'Entrèves, *op. cit.* p. 60.   [2] Nardi, *op. cit.* p. 285.

tion to steer clear, so far as possible, of the intricate problem of the chronology of Dante's work, to deal with which even a further lecture would probably prove inadequate. I will confine myself, therefore, to stating that while many critics hold that the *Comedy* was written entirely in the last seven years of the poet's life, and after the *Monarchia* had been completed, there are equally good, if not better, grounds for maintaining that part of the *Comedy* was written earlier, and that the composition of the poem was interrupted for a time when Dante turned to the political treatise; in which case (and this is a possibility one has to take into account) one must conclude that Dante could hardly have expounded conflicting sentiments at the same time.

But even without resorting to the aid of more or less problematic chronological considerations, there seem to be strong reasons to believe that Dante never altered his views at any stage during his exile from Florence, and that the *Comedy* accepts the scheme outlined in the *Monarchia*. It ought to be borne in mind that the poem and the treatise are very different in their subject and nature, and were intended for very different purposes. Examining things from a different angle, dealing with another subject, do not of themselves mean contradicting what one has written elsewhere. In the *Monarchia* Dante addresses himself to reason, in the *Comedy* to imagination as well as to reason; the *Monarchia* focuses the reader's attention on the regeneration of the Empire, the *Comedy* deals with the regeneration both of the Empire and of the Church. The *Monarchia* is preoccupied with the happiness of mankind on earth, the *Comedy* with man's journey towards eternal salvation; that is to say, the *Monarchia* deals scientifically with one particular aspect of mankind's pilgrimage on earth, whereas the *Comedy* deals poetically with the whole of this theme. It is inevitable, therefore, that the emphasis should be elsewhere, that the tone should not be the same; but it does not follow that the thought has changed. And, indeed, one can find in the *Comedy* indications that Dante has not jettisoned the idea of the autonomy of the Empire. In fact, the overriding need for the independence of the Empire from the Church in the political sphere is restated in this work. Examples that come to mind are the celebration of the glories of the Imperial Eagle in the sixth canto of the *Paradiso*, where the historical material and the theoretical assumptions of the *Convivio* and of the *Monarchia* are still held to be valid, and are re-expounded in a light of poetic, indeed epic, splendour; the seat reserved in the Empyrean Heaven for Henry VII, that incarnation, as he must have come to be regarded, of the principle of imperial autonomy (*Par.* xxx, 133–8); and, amidst other passages in the three *cantiche*, the intimation to the clergy to allow Caesar to sit in the saddle (*Purg.* vi, 91–2); and those nostalgic lines (*Purg.* xvi, 106–8) of Marco Lombardo, which restate the distinction between the 'duo fines' of mankind, and, therefore, between the two guides pre-ordained for the two aims:

> Soleva Roma, che 'l buon mondo feo,
>   due soli aver, che l'una e l'altra strada
>   facean vedere, e del mondo e di deo.★

★ 'Rome, that made the world well disposed [that is to receive the Christian faith], was used to have two Suns, that pointed out the one and the other way, that of the world, and that of God.'

These examples suggest that the affirmation of the two aims of mankind and of the means to achieve them, a distinction that was useful for the exact definition of the respective spheres of the temporal and of the spiritual power, did not imply for Dante a denial of the subordination of reason to faith; it implied that the authority of the Emperor derives directly from God, and not from the Pope; it implied that different means are suited to different ends. But it did not exclude a co-operation, or even a subordination 'in aliquo', for, he emphasized, earthly happiness is to be seen 'quodam modo' in the light of eternal happiness.

Having made it clear why I believe that Dante held consistently to his political views, I must now attempt a brief assessment. A question that faces the reader of the *Monarchia* is whether the scheme it outlines should be regarded as a dream, or as a sound piece of practical politics. It is also, perhaps, the hardest to answer. Indeed, it is impossible to give a clear-cut answer, as is so often the case with the many-sided problems raised by Dante's thought. The very nature of the book is such that it hovers all the time between reality and utopia. Dante's monarch, it has been pointed out, was a personified abstraction, a symbol surrounded by some nebulous and fantastic aura.[1] It harked back to a situation in European politics which had ceased to exist a long time before, probably at the moment of the break-up of the Carolingian Empire, and certainly at the death of Frederick II. Indeed, with the rise of great national states, the Empire was no longer even the greatest

[1] See, for example, A. D'Ancona, 'Il "De Monarchia"', *Scritti danteschi* (Florence, G. C. Sansoni, 1913), p. 337.

power in Europe. The very city-states of Italy, which in theory still recognized the Emperor as the source of all laws, in practice were jealously determined to safeguard their sovereignty. Dante, it has often been implied, was trying to resurrect a corpse. Yet this negative view of the *Monarchia* leaves Henry VII completely out of account. Henry VII had attempted exactly what Dante had longed for, the restoration of the universal Empire, and had backed up his attempt with official pronouncements embodying a conception of the relationship between Empire and Papacy which coincides very closely with the ideas expounded in the *Monarchia*. Had Henry's bid for the re-establishment of the universal Empire any chance of succeeding? Or was it the scheme of an idealist, doomed to failure from the start? Whatever view one takes of Henry and his luckless Italian campaign, it would be wrong to disregard the atmosphere of expectancy and anticipation which preceded and accompanied, in the whole of Italy, the journey of this Emperor who described himself as a 'Rex Pacificus', the feeling that he might yet succeed in his intent, which persisted even when the ailing Henry marched against the King of Naples a few days before his death: a feeling which made the hearts of his supporters fill with hope, and those of his foes with fear. The imperial idea, even if events had irrevocably made it unrealistic, lingered on strongly in Italy, and, fanned by the persistent tradition of the glory of the Roman Empire, by the continuity that was seen between Roman and Italian history and by the concept of the Empire as the sole source of law, still retained many followers. This is the background against which the *Monarchia* was conceived; and indeed, although nobody had ever argued so closely and worked out so exhaustively the theory of a universal monarchy, the nature of the authority of the Emperor had been a widely discussed topical subject, and many of the arguments accepted or refuted by Dante had figured prominently in the pronouncements of Boniface, of Philippe le Bel, of Clement V and of Henry.

That Dante had shared the sanguine hopes awakened by Henry's expedition to Italy is abundantly proved, above all, by the three epistles written in those years; and it seems highly likely that the events of that fateful period induced him to give organic form to ideas that had been maturing for a long time, perhaps even from the time when Boniface had solemnly and repeatedly defined his views on the authority of the Church. The many links between the *Monarchia* and the documents which had been issued by the chanceries of the Emperor, of the Pope, of the King of France and of the King of Naples support the view that it was written between 1312 and 1314. It would be a mistake, however, to conclude that it was a pamphlet prepared for a certain occasion. The fact that it contains no explicit reference to current events or personalities makes it stand outside time. Nor should it be assumed that Dante deluded himself into thinking that the millennium was round the corner. He firmly believed that the universal monarchy was pre-ordained to come, but in God's own time. He was no visionary who would imprison his scheme in rigid formulas, or imagine that men could be persuaded to see and accept the truth overnight. The Emperor he envisaged was not expected to achieve automatically the miracle of peace and justice, as the compactness of Dante's reasoning might sometimes lead us to think. He well knew how much virtue and how much blood the establishment of the Empire cost the Romans over many centuries, and had seen how cities and princes and kings had conspired in his own time to impede the progress of the Emperor. The *Monarchia*, therefore, defines the conditions that are ideally favourable for the advent of the monarchy, and the haven of peace and freedom and justice in this mortal 'areola' is one towards which the Roman Prince must strive with all his strength. It is a 'signum ad quod maxime debet intendere [...] Romanus Princeps' (*Mon.* III, xvi, 11).

Even having ascertained that Dante saw the restoration of the universal Empire as a gradual process, we are not any nearer to deciding whether the *Monarchia* belongs to the realm of dreams or of practical politics; for stating these two alternatives is framing the problem in the wrong way. In the *Monarchia* there is, really, no question of practical politics. For all its resounding with the echoes of bitterly fought struggles that were firmly rooted in the politics of the day, for all its drawing its substance from the experience of Dante's life, the *Monarchia* is not essentially a political work in the sense that is generally given to this expression. It is not concerned with a reform of the way of governing this or that state, but rather with the search, on a rational and philosophical plane, for the ideal conditions ordained by God to secure happiness during man's journey through life. It is the result not of a profound knowledge of political affairs, but of a profound faith. Since Dante could not believe that justice would not ultimately triumph, he must believe that what was so manifestly willed by God would come true, if only men could be taught to see it. If only the evil of the Donation of Constantine could be undone, if the Emperor resumed his proper function and the temporal power were recognized as independent from the spiritual, all would be well. A strong optimism is the mainspring of the book, a confidence that 'la cagion che 'l mondo ha fatto reo' (*Purg.* XVI, 104), the confusion of the two powers, and its principal cause, covetousness, can be removed, and that an Emperor placed above the worries of everyday life and beyond the reach of greed can be really free, and can apply his energies to governing well and to furthering the achievement of man's purpose in life. The same sense of mission that sustained Dante while he wrote the *Comedy* is present in the *Monarchia*. It is this that sets the book apart from the political literature of its time. Dante was aware that he had undertaken a task 'al quale han posto mano e cielo e terra'* (*Par.* XXV, 2), that of preparing mankind for the coming of God's envoy, a Greyhound (*Inf.* I, 101), who would rid the world of avarice, the root of all its evils. His labours were meant for the advantage of posterity ('posteris prolaborare', *Mon.* I, i, 1) and were strengthened by the conviction that he was revealing truths whose discovery had never been attempted before ('intemptatas ab aliis ostendere veritates', *Mon.* I, i, 3). His vigils, he averred, were to bring benefit to the world, and to him the glory of having been the first to carry to completion such a mighty enterprise (*Mon.* I, i, 5). If the

* 'To which both Heaven and Earth have set their hand.'

Monarchia had been merely a political pamphlet, a piece of Ghibelline propaganda, its impact at the time when it was written, over the centuries and now would have been far less. But in this work (as in all his other works) Dante's heart was as involved as his mind, and his passionate feelings occasionally burst through the serried ranks of syllogisms: for instance, when Dante commiserates with mankind at the thought of the seamless tunic (the unity of the Empire) torn by the Donation of Constantine, the cause and at the same time the result of greed: 'O genus humanum, quantis procellis atque iacturis quantisque naufragiis agitari te necesse est!'* (*Mon.* I, xvi, 4); or when he is filled with horrified sorrow at the painful spectacle of kings and princes agreeing in this alone, that they should oppose their Lord and their anointed one, the Roman Prince (*Mon.* II, i, 3). It is moving to stumble upon such spontaneous cries from the heart. The austere reasoning which is the framework of the book is then seen not merely as an intellectually satisfying instrument for the pursuit of theoretical truths, but as an intimately felt, warm, passionate expression of convictions that have matured as a result both of their author's meditations upon ancient and more recent writers and of what life had taught him.

The *Monarchia* has been read, discussed, praised and abominated for the last six and a half centuries. I do not think that this is due only to the fact that it provides a key to the understanding of the *Comedy* and that, therefore, it shines with the reflected glory of an incomparable work of

---

* 'Wretched mankind, amidst what storms and misfortunes and shipwrecks it is your fate to be tossed!'

poetry. Although it is steeped in the ways of thinking of the Middle Ages, the *Monarchia* retains a vitality of its own. Even recently it has been the subject of a polemic fought, if not exactly for the same reasons that lay behind the debates of the fourteenth century, at least for similar ones.[1] Thus the *Monarchia* can be seen to have attracted, and to continue to attract today, approval and animosity, because Dante has embodied in it a certain outlook on life, or, more precisely, an outlook on the way in which men's affairs, and particularly political affairs, should be arranged. Although any attempts to identify this outlook too closely with trends of thought of our times are bound to be misleading, it could, perhaps, be described as internationalism rather than nationalism, laicism rather than theocracy, in the arrangement of human affairs, an internationalism (and it is on this note that I would like to conclude) based on that noble and ever attractive ideal—a 'universalis civilitas humani generis' (*Mon.* I, ii, 8). It is for this ideal that Dante strove, for the achievement of universal peace, freedom and justice for mankind conceived as a single social unit. Such a motive adds a quality of timelessness to his message.

[1] M. Maccarrone, 'Il terzo libro della "Monarchia"', *Studi Danteschi*, XXXIII (1955), pp. 5–142; B. Nardi, 'Intorno ad una nuova interpretazione del terzo libro della "Monarchia" dantesca', *Dal 'Convivio' alla 'Commedia'* (Rome, Istituto Storico Italiano per il Medio Evo, 1960), pp. 151–313.

DANTE'S VIEWS ON LANGUAGE

J. CREMONA

Gianfranco Contini lucidly brought out a constant in Dante's personality when he said that in the poet's writing technical reflexion continually catches up with poetry and that the active writing of poetry is constantly associated with the theoretical study of style.[1] This same double approach may be traced in Dante's attitude to language. Here, his interest was clearly twofold: that of the poet, for whom language is the essential medium; that of the philosopher, of the historian, perhaps even of the political thinker, for whom language is a basic object of study. No wonder then if we find Dante preoccupied with questions of language throughout his life—questions that not only concern the concrete language he used (quite apart from stylistic considerations), but also questions on the nature and function, on the organization and history of language in general. Reflexions on these topics may be found scattered throughout his work, from the *Vita Nuova* to the last *cantica* of the *Divine Comedy*. But it is chiefly in a special work devoted to the subject (albeit unfinished) that the poet's thoughts are revealed to their fullest extent: the

[1] 'Una costante della personalità dantesca...questo perpetuo sopraggiungere della riflessione tecnica accanto alla poesia, quest'associazione di concreto poetare e d'intelligenza stilistica' (Dante Alighieri, *Rime*, a cura di Gianfranco Contini, Torino, 1946, p. 10). See also C. Grayson, 'Dante e la prosa volgare', *Il Verri*, IX (1963), 12.

De Vulgari Eloquentia. In its finished form the work was obviously meant to be a treatise on the art of writing in the vernacular (quite how wide its scope was to be is a matter of some debate). But the whole of book I, the only completed section, is devoted to an exposition of the origin and nature of human language and to a picture of the linguistic situation of Europe with particular reference to the Italy of his time.

Language for Dante was not simply a gift from God to Man. It was the natural consequence of the humanity of Man. For Dante Man is essentially a created being, living in society and endowed with reason. Man is not moved by natural instinct but by reason, and it is this that makes every man an individual, different from his neighbours (*DVE*, I, iii, I). This rational, social and differentiated basis of human life makes it necessary that Man should be able to communicate with his neighbours by means of a rational system of signs built upon a concrete physical basis. In this respect he is placed exactly half-way between the angelic and the animal forms of existence. Angels, being wholly spiritual, are wholly able to compenetrate each other's minds and need, therefore, no special means of communication; indeed it could be said that they do not need communication. Animals on the other hand, moved as they are entirely by natural instincts common to all and possessing no reason, have nothing to communicate. When they belong to the same species, a kind of introspection is sufficient: ' . . . they are able to know those acts and passions that are in their fellows by those that are in themselves'* (*DVE*, I, ii, 5);

---

* 'Nam omnibus eiusdem speciei sunt iidem actus et passiones; et sic possunt per proprios alienos cognoscere.'

they thus appear to be undifferentiated. When they belong to different species, no communication is necessary since there is no society. Men therefore partake both of animals and of angels: they share with animals the limitations imposed by their bodies and thus communication between individuals must be physically based; they share with angels some of their intellectual nature and this gives rise to the need for communication. This closely knit, scholastically conducted argument is typical of the working of Dante's mind and faithfully reflects his hierarchical view of nature; we shall see it operating in several instances.

We have unfortunately not the time to go into the inessentials of this theory as worked out by Dante: the linguistic position of devils, for example, or that of talking animals, such as Balaam's ass or Ovid's magpies. But I should like to stress the very high place given to language among man's activities. It is among those 'operations proper to the rational soul, on which the divine light most directly shines'* (*Con.* III, vii, 8). This high regard is expressed indirectly in a number of ways. When the question is raised as to which of the two first human beings was the first to speak, Dante feels strongly that, although *Genesis* makes Eve speak first (in answer to the serpent), '...it is reasonable to believe that the man must have been the first speaker, for it is not fitting to think that such a noble act should have first been performed by a woman and not by a man'† (*DVE*, I, iv, 3). Later, there comes the question

* '...quelle operazioni che sono proprie de l'anima razionale, dove la divina luce più espeditamente raggia; cioè nel parlare e ne li atti che reggimenti e portamenti sogliono esser chiamati.'

† 'Sed quanquam mulier in scriptis prius inveniatur locuta, rationa-

as to who were the participants in the first dialogue; the answer could only be the most noble combination: Adam and his Maker. Or again the question as to which was the first word used by the first speaker: this could only have been the most noble word of all, *El*, the word for God in Adam's language.

The substance of Dante's thoughts on the nature and function of language is, for the most part, though originally and finely presented, that of patristic and scholastic theology and philosophy: as expressed in Augustine, Isidore and Thomas Aquinas when concerned with Biblical exegesis; as formulated by the scholastic grammarians when concerned with grammatical (linguistic) theory.[1] The same cannot be said, however, of his views on the history and characteristics of language, or of the picture he sketches of the linguistic situation of contemporary Italy. Here he is at his most original and innovating or, to use adjectives employed by Alfred Ewert, striking, intriguing and epoch-making.[2]

The double nature of Man—spiritual and physical—entails as a consequence a double nature to the linguistic

bile tamen est ut hominem prius locutum fuisse credamus; et inconvenienter putatur tam egregium humani generis actum prius a femina quam a viro profluisse.'

[1] See P. Rotta, *La filosofia del linguaggio nella Patristica e nella Scolastica* (Torino, 1909); R. H. Robins, *Ancient and Medieval Grammatical Theory in Europe* (London, 1951); B. Nardi, *Dante e la cultura medievale* (Bari, 1942) (ch. IV, 'Il linguaggio'); B. Terracini, 'Natura e origine del linguaggio umano nel "De Vulgari Eloquentia"', *Pagine e appunti di linguistica storica* (Firenze, 1957). See also A. Marigo's edition of the *De Vulgari Eloquentia* (Firenze, 1957), *passim*.

[2] A. Ewert, 'Dante's Theory of Language', *The Modern Language Review*, XXXV (1940), 357.

141

sign. The sign is both rational and sensible, that is, percep-
tible by the senses. But let me quote in full, for Dante is
very explicit on this point:

It was therefore necessary that in order to communicate its
concepts, mankind should dispose of some sign that was both
rational and sensible ('rationale signum et sensuale'); for since
it was to receive from reason and to hand over to reason, it
had to be rational; and as nothing can be transferred from one
reason to another except by means of a sensible medium, it
had to be sensible. For if it were only rational, it could not
bridge the gap; and if it were only sensible, it could neither
receive from reason nor hand over to reason. It is this very
sign which is the noble subject of my discourse: partly sensible
in so far as it consists of sound, and partly rational in so far as
it is seen to signify something arbitrarily ('ad placitum').★

(*DVE*, I, iii, 2–3.)

We have here the bones of a conceptual theory of
meaning, and such theories were in fact current among
medieval grammarians of the late thirteenth century.[1]
From what Dante says, there appears to be a direct and
intimate connexion between sound and meaning, and this
connexion is of a mental nature. Such a relation is highly
reminiscent of de Saussure's theory of the linguistic sign.

---

[1] For example, Siger de Courtrai (see Robins, *op. cit.* p. 81).

★ 'Oportuit ergo genus humanum ad comunicandum inter se con-
ceptiones suas aliquod rationale signum et sensuale habere; quia, cum
de ratione accipere habeat et in rationem portare, rationale esse oportuit;
cumque de una ratione in aliam nichil deferri possit nisi per medium
sensuale, sensuale esse oportuit; quare, si tantum rationale esset, per-
transire non posset; si tantum sensuale, nec a ratione accipere, nec in
rationem deponere potuisset. Hoc equidem signum est ipsum subiec-
tum nobile de quo loquimur: nam sensuale quid est, in quantum
sonus est; rationale vero, in quantum aliquid significare videtur ad
placitum.'

Dante's Views on Language

What is perhaps of greater interest, however, is concentrated in the final phrase of the quotation I have just given: the linguistic sign is seen to signify something 'ad placitum'. I understand this to mean that the relation between the phonic form and the concept is an arbitrary one. Here again we have a foretaste of de Saussure: in this case of the Swiss scholar's insistence on the arbitrariness of the linguistic sign. The phrase is, in fact, a clear enough statement of Dante's position in relation to the old classical controversy on whether language is 'natural' or 'conventional' in nature, motivated or arbitrary (the φύσις/ νόμος debate, as outlined in Plato's *Cratylus*). That is, in simple terms, whether there is or is not a causal connexion between the form and the meaning of a word. The 'natural' solution, favoured by the 'Platonists', was rejected in favour of the 'conventional' by the more 'Aristotelian' scholastic grammarians of the thirteenth century, particularly by St Thomas. Here Dante is echoing the latter's words.

The phrase 'ad placitum' or its equivalent 'beneplacitum' is repeated a number of times in the *De Vulgari Eloquentia* with reference to language, but the notion of arbitrariness receives a final blessing from the mouth of Adam himself, in the *Paradiso*:

> Opera naturale è ch'uom favella;
> ma così o così, natura lascia
> poi fare a voi, secondo che v'abbella.*
>
> (*Par.* XXVI, 130–2.)

---

* 'It is a work of nature that man should speak, but whether in this way or that nature then leaves you to follow your own pleasure' (transl. by J. D. Sinclair).

The faculty of speech is natural to man. But the form which speech takes on the lips of men is left to man, 'secondo che v'abbella': 'ad placitum'. If there were a 'natural' connexion between, say, a word and its meaning, the signifier and the signified, then the 'ad placitum' would become a largely meaningless phrase.

Yet there has been considerable discussion on this very question, chiefly because of a passage in the *Vita Nuova* where Dante seems to take a more 'Platonic' view of the problem. I am referring to the place where Dante praises the name of personified love, 'Amore': 'the name "Amore" is so sweet to the ear, that it seems to me impossible that its operation on most things could be other than sweet, since names [nouns?] follow the things that are named, as it is written: "Nomina sunt consequentia rerum"'* (*VN*, xiii, 4).

At first sight this passage does seem to imply a certain motivation, at least in this word; as a result the meaning of the whole sentence and particularly of the final phrase, 'nomina sunt consequentia rerum', has been much commented on, though not always with great clarity. Setting aside the fact that it is found in a comparatively youthful work when Dante's thoughts on this subject may not have been fully matured, and the fact too that *Amore* is quoted here as a proper noun, it has been found possible to read somewhat different meanings in both the Italian and the Latin phrases, meanings that do not clash so radically with

* 'lo nome d'Amore è sì dolce a udire, che impossibile mi pare che la sua propria operazione sia ne le più cose altro che dolce, con ciò sia cosa che li nomi seguitino le nominate cose, sì come è scritto: "Nomina sunt consequentia rerum."'

what Dante says in the later work.[1] The probable meaning of the second part of the sentence is that *Amore* sounds so sweet because the notion it is associated with *is* so sweet: the relation is one of association, not of cause and effect. It is hardly surprising that in a poet sound and meaning should be closely associated: there is explicit evidence for this when, in a later chapter of the *De Vulgari Eloquentia*, Dante describes which words are appropriate to the highest style and which are not (*DVE*, II, vii). This does not mean, however, that such a principle can be erected into a general theory on the origin and formation of words. A further argument against a belief in a 'natural' origin or genesis of the word 'Amore' is the fact that when Dante seeks to prove the common parentage of the three Romance languages of *oc*, *oïl* and *sì*, he cites this very word 'amore', common to all three languages, as a convincing argument. Such an argument would fall to the ground if the sound of the word was to any extent 'natural' or motivated.

We come now to the *forma locutionis*, to the formal organization of language into an articulate whole, to grammar, in fact. Here, too, Dante is not particularly original and moves well within the grammatical and logical tradition of his time.[2] Three levels are distinguished and they are presented to us in a descending order of analysis (*DVE*, I, vi, 4). I prefer to give them in an ascending

---

[1] For example, Nardi, *op. cit.* pp. 149–55; A. Pagliaro, 'I "primissima signa" nella dottrina linguistica di Dante', *Nuovi saggi di critica semantica* (Messina–Firenze, 1956), pp. 239–46. Professor E. R. Vincent, on the other hand, sees a 'Platonic' meaning in the sentence (see 'Dante's Choice of Words', *Italian Studies*, x, 1955, pp. 5–8).

[2] Cf. Pagliaro, *op. cit.* p. 226.

order as their articulation is then apprehended more clearly. They are: the *prolatio constructionis*, the *constructio vocabulorum* and the *vocabula rerum*. The *prolatio constructionis* appears to correspond to what we would call, in traditional linguistic terminology, the phonetics, the morphology and the syntax of agreement: under this one heading, we find most of what we traditionally call grammar. The *constructio vocabulorum*, on the other hand, corresponds roughly to what we would call the order of words in the sentence, the syntax of arrangement. Finally, the *vocabula rerum* correspond to the vocabulary, the mass of lexical items including, despite the name, relational items (pronouns, articles, etc.) elsewhere defined separately as *vocabula necessaria*.

The most interesting feature of this tripartite arrangement is perhaps the fact that these three levels of analysis appear to be distributed between the two natural planes, the rational and the sensible: the *prolationes constructionis* and the *vocabula rerum* belong to the sensible plane; the *constructio vocabulorum* to the rational.[1] Thus what we have called the syntax of arrangement, the *constructio vocabulorum*, being rational, is also logical and therefore non-arbitrary but motivated. Moreover, being logical, it is structured and constant and will not vary appreciably from language to language: it is dependent upon the concept of order; whereas the *prolationes* (the greater part of grammar) and the *vocabula*, being sensible, are arbitrary and accidental. It is in these last two levels that languages differ from one another and change in the course

[1] Cf. Terracini, *op. cit.* p. 242.

of time. This is implicitly stated in the passage describing
the multiplicity of languages to be found in the world after
the destruction of the tower of Babel: ' . . . the whole world
is divided into many different *prolationes et vocabula*'
(*DVE*, I, i, 4). No mention is made here of a confusion
of *constructiones*. In the *Convivio*, however, all three are
said to vary in the course of time: ' . . . some words, some
declensions, some constructions are now in use which
were not in the past, and many existed in the past which
will occur again . . .'* (*Con.* II, xiii, 10). This passage may
have been written earlier than the *De Vulgari Eloquentia*[1]
and may mirror a less definitive stage in the development of the poet's thought.

There is little further analysis on the linguistic plane
beyond the tripartite division we have been examining.
What remarks there are in the *De Vulgari* on the phonetics,
the syntax or the vocabulary of Italian or Latin are written
entirely from the point of view of style (*DVE*, II, vi and vii),
and but for a few exceptions show no particular analytical
linguistic insight. It is clear that Dante's approach to
language, even in the first book of the *De Vulgari Eloquentia*,
is basically a stylistic one, that of the writer: far more subtle
than that of contemporary grammarians when it came to
appreciating the living reality of his own language, but
fundamentally incurious when it came to its mechanism,
to pulling it apart. There are, however, a few highly per-
ceptive remarks particularly on the subject of vocabulary.

---

* ' . . . certi vocaboli, certe declinazioni, certe construzioni sono in uso
che già non furono, e molte già furono che ancor saranno. . . .'

[1] See G. Vinay, 'Richerche sul "De Vulgari Eloquentia"', *Giornale
Storico della Letteratura Italiana*, CXXXVI (1959), 239.

10-2

The Mind of Dante

The 'open' nature of the vocabulary of a language (even that of Latin) is clearly hinted at in a complex simile in the *Convivio* (II, xiii, 10).[1] And when the vocabulary of Italian is examined to describe which words are suitable to the highest style, the individual items are classified and defined according to three criteria: context, meaning and form, in descending order of importance.[2]

We have so far been examining the more descriptive aspects of Dante's conception of language and we have seen that, taken as a whole, it has few claims to originality. A very different conclusion must be reached, however, when we come to determine the historical aspects of his approach to the subject.

Language, as we have seen, is of divine origin. But Dante gives us two versions of the way in which language was created: one in the *De Vulgari Eloquentia* and a second in the *Paradiso*. In the first, Adam received from God in the Garden of Eden not merely the faculty of speech but the actual *forma* of a language, that is, its basic structure and a given form: '...we say that a certain form of speech was created by God together with the first soul'* (*DVE*, I, vi, 4). Here Dante appears to be more definite than St Thomas, who shows some hesitation on whether Adam was given a fully developed, ready-made language or more

[1] 'E queste due proprietadi hae la Gramatica: ché, per la sua infinitade, li raggi de la ragione in essa non si terminano, in parte spezialmente de li vocabuli...'.

[2] See especially A. Ewert, 'Dante's Theory of Diction', *Annual Bulletin of the Modern Humanities Research Association*, XXXI (1959), 21–8.

* '...dicimus certam formam locutionis a Deo cum anima prima concreatam fuisse.'

simply the faculty to speak. Dante opts for the first of the two alternatives, and it is in fact consonant with one of the main themes of the book, the nobility of the vernacular, the natural language.[1] This primitive language was of course Hebrew. And it is a 'language of grace', which remained with the whole of mankind without changing down to the catastrophe of Babel. And after Babel it lived on, unchanged, as the language of the children of Heber, the Hebrews, who took no part in the building of the tower; in this way the Redeemer did not have to avail himself of a language of confusion but was able to speak the language of grace.

The contradiction inherent in this version of the story is worth pointing out since, for one thing, it supports the contention that the treatise shows signs of hasty composition. If Hebrew was the language of grace, then Hebrew is the most noble of the languages on earth. And the foremost quality of the nature of Hebrew, according to this version, is that it is unchanging and permanent, unlike all the other vernaculars to be found on earth. This would hardly tell in favour of the vernaculars, especially when compared to Latin, among whose qualities was also that of permanence, received at the hands of art. We should remember here that one of the main themes of the *De Vulgari Eloquentia* is Dante's contention: 'nobilior est vulgaris', the greater nobility of the vernacular as compared with Latin.

It is therefore hardly surprising to find a second version of the events in the *Paradiso*, this time from the mouth of

[1] Cf. Marigo, *op. cit.* p. lix.

Adam himself. I have already quoted part of it; here is the whole of the relevant passage:

> La lingua ch'io parlai fu tutta spenta
> innanzi che all'ovra inconsummabile
> fosse la gente di Nembròt attenta;
> ché nullo effetto mai razionabile,
> per lo piacere uman che rinnovella
> seguendo il cielo, sempre fu durabile.
> Opera naturale è ch'uom favella;
> ma così o così, natura lascia
> poi fare a voi, secondo che v'abbella.
> Pria ch'io scendessi a l'infernale ambascia,
> *I* s'appellava in terra il sommo bene
> onde vien la letizia che mi fascia;
> e *EL* si chiamò poi: e ciò convene,
> ché l'uso de' mortali è come fronda
> in ramo, che sen va e altra vene.*
>
> (*Par.* XXVI, 124–38.)

Adam seems to give us a somewhat different version of the genesis of human language in the well-known *terzina* 'Opera natural è ch'uom favella...'. In this version it would appear that the faculty of speech alone was given to Adam and not the *forma*. More significant, however, is the recantation of the earlier doctrine of the immutability of Adamitic language. According to this second version

* 'The tongue I spoke was all extinct before Nimrod's race gave their mind to the unaccomplishable task; for no product whatever of reason—since human choice is renewed with the course of heaven—can last forever. It is a work of nature that man should speak, but whether in this way or that nature then leaves you to follow your own pleasure. Before I descended to the anguish of Hell the Supreme Good from whom comes the joy that swathes me was named *I* on earth, and later He was called *EL*; and that is fitting, for the usage of mortals is like a leaf on a branch, which goes and another comes' (transl. by J. D. Sinclair).

language began to change right from its beginnings, presumably at the Fall, since no product of reason can last for ever. And to hammer this point home with a concrete example, we are given a brief history of the very first word said to have been pronounced by the lips of man: the word for God himself. During Adam's lifetime it was *I*, presumably the first letter of the name Yahweh; later it became *El*, the Hebrew word for God. The change occurred not through regular phonetic evolution (the notion appears to have been unknown to Dante), but by substitution—like the shedding of a leaf and the opening of a new one.

The theme of the variability of human language both in time and space constantly recurs in Dante. We have just seen it in the *Paradiso*. We find it too in the *Convivio* (I, v, 9–10); but it is best formulated in a finely written passage of the *De Vulgari Eloquentia* (I, ix, 6–10). Here it is stated that no language can be lasting in time or continuous in space, for man is a highly unstable and variable animal; in this respect language is placed on a par with human customs and fashions ('sicut alia que nostra sunt, puta mores et habitus'). Dante goes on to affirm that as a result a contemporary Pavian would find it hard to understand a resurrected Pavian of old, and that it was only the gradualness of linguistic change and the brevity of human life that blinded some men to this fact.

We come now to the catastrophe of Babel. As we would expect, this is given a central and crucial place in Dante's brief history of the human language. It is the parting of the ways and it is told in one of the most compelling chapters of the *De Vulgari* (I, vii). The main story does not depart to any extent from Genesis; but we do find in it the addition of two significant details which vividly fill in the picture and give us much insight into Dante's view of language.

The first concerns the actual division of the primitive 'language of grace' into the many 'languages of confusion'—we must remember that we are still at the stage where Dante believed that the primitive language had remained unchanged. The way in which the various languages of confusion arose at Babel is not clearly stated in Genesis or in the patristic literature on the subject. Dante interprets the division as parting not individual from individual, not family or 'gens' from other families or 'gentes', but as dividing one occupational group from the others, according to their trade. There resulted as many languages as there were trades: one for the architects, another for the quarrymen, yet another for the dressers of stone, and so on. This is a most original view of the division and it is difficult not to see in it a reflexion of the political division of contemporary Florence into twelve major and nine minor 'Arti', or Guilds. The division seems to indicate that Dante had observed that in a given society, linguistic cleavage does tend to occur along occupational lines and to produce jargons. Such a view immediately reminds the linguist of Antoine Meillet's opposition of *langue commune* to *langues de groupe* and of the role of this opposition in initiating linguistic change.[1]

---

[1] G. Vinay (*op. cit.* p. 386) interprets the relevant passage somewhat differently: the cleavage does not occur according to the trades but to the actual acts being performed at the time of the catastrophe.

Dante's Views on Language

The second elaboration Dante works into the story of Babel concerns the amount of confusion injected into the various languages. A kind of hierarchy is established, according to which the degree of confusion introduced varies in proportion to the degree of responsibility of the relevant trade: the more responsible the trade, the greater the confusion, '. . . the more highly skilled their work, the ruder and the more barbarian their speech'* (*DVE*, I, vii, 7). And to the most responsible of all, the instigator himself, Nimrod, there befell the ghastliest language, unintelligible to all, the very negation of communication. This theme is repeated in *Inf.* XXXI:

> questi è Nembròt, per lo cui mal coto
> pur un linguaggio nel mondo non s'usa.
> Lasciamlo stare e non parliamo a voto;
> ché così è a lui ciascun linguaggio
> come 'l suo ad altrui, ch'a nullo è noto.†
>
> (*Inf.* XXXI, 77-81.)

What the linguistic nature of the confusion was, we are not told explicitly, except that it affected the *prolationes constructionis* and the *vocabula rerum* (*DVE*, I, i, 4) as we have already seen, that it involved the forgetting in some measure of the primitive language of grace and that some form of reconstruction subsequently took place (*DVE*, I, ix, 6).

An interesting implication derives from an acceptance of the Babel episode together with Dante's second opinion

---

* '. . . quanto excellentius exercebant, tanto rudius nunc barbariusque locuntur.'

† 'This is Nimrod, through whose wicked device the world is not of one sole speech. Let us leave him there and not talk in vain, for every language is to him as his to others, which is known to none' (transl. by J. D. Sinclair).

on the instability of the pre-Babelic language. If Babel is to retain the full significance it possesses in Genesis, that of a divine punishment comparable in importance to the Flood, then we are forced to postulate either that the pre-Babelic language evolved only with time and not with place or, alternatively, that mankind did not disperse before the building of the tower. The implication of such a deduction struck Bruno Nardi as being potentially quasi-heretical.[1] Dante does write in one passage of the *De Vulgari* that he has strong reasons to believe that mankind was united in place (and therefore in language), until the confusion of tongues (*DVE*, I, viii, 1); and Genesis explicitly states: ' ... confusum est labium universae terrae, et inde dispersit eos Dominus super faciem cunctarum regionum' (XI, 9). But Dante is uncertain on this point, and the alternative of an earlier dispersal is restated a few lines later without a clear position being taken. The implication, in any case, would only become valid after the writing of the *Paradiso*.

The immediate post-Babelic history of the languages of Europe as found in the *De Vulgari Eloquentia* is derived mainly from Isidore's *Etymologiae*.[2] Dante describes the peoples who were to inhabit Europe, the Japhetic peoples, as possessing a triform language ('ydioma tripharium'), the division having presumably occurred at Babel *in posse* if not *in esse*. Dante's thoughts in this passage are a little obscure and there is a marked contrast with the clarity of the rest of the exposition. At any rate, three linguistically differentiated groups of peoples settled over Europe. One occupied the whole of northern Europe and may be recog-

---

[1] Nardi, *op. cit.* pp. 174–5.   [2] Cf. Marigo, *op. cit.* p. 47.

nized from the word they use for the affirmative particle: *jo*; they include the *Sclavones*, the *Ungari*, the *Teutonici*, the *Saxones* and the *Anglici*. Another group, the *Greci*, occupied Eastern Europe and part of Asia. The third group, of more concern to him, occupied Southern Europe and spoke a language to which Dante again refers by the term 'ydioma tripharium'; this is the direct ancestor of what we now call the Romance languages.

The originality of Dante's views on the subsequent history of this second 'ydioma tripharium' or common Romance is expressly stated by the poet himself: '...my intention is to enquire into matters concerning which I cannot lean upon the authority of anyone'* (*DVE*, I, ix, 1). It is at this point that in order to explain the multiplicity of forms the *ydioma tripharium* took within Romance territory, Dante insists upon the inevitability of change in human speech in a passage of extraordinary modernity. As the result of this instability the *ydioma tripharium* came to be differentiated into a set of three groups of vernaculars, which Dante labelled according to the word for 'yes' in each of the groups: *oc*, *oïl* and *sì*.

The first group, the *lingua oc*, is identified with a people Dante calls the *Yspani*, which includes the inhabitants of Southern France and of Spain; it is worth noting, in fact, that the early Catalan poets wrote their verses in *langue d'oc*. It is worth noting, too, that Dante's main point of reference is the literary language of the area concerned. Also that he does not seem to have knowledge of the

---

* '...cum inquirere intendamus de hiis in quibus nullius auctoritate fulcimur.'

considerable body of lyric poetry written in Galician-Portuguese. His enumeration of the Romance group of vernaculars differs considerably from the one to be found in Raimbautz de Vaqueiras's *Descort*, written about a century earlier and where no less than five distinct Romance vernaculars are given: Provençal, Italian, French, Gascon and Galician-Portuguese. It is quite possible, too, that Dante's well known predilection for the number three may have affected his analysis.

The second group, the *lingua oïl*, is identified with the *Franci*, and the third, the *lingua sì*, with the *Latini*, the name Dante regularly gives to the inhabitants 'del bel paese là dove 'l sì suona'* (*Inf.* XXXIII, 80).

We may note at this point that at no stage in the *De Vulgari Eloquentia* does Dante use specific adjectives to describe the various Romance vernaculars or, for that matter, the vernaculars of Italy. The word *vulgaris* or occasionally *lingua* is found accompanied when the need arises by the ethnic name in the genitive or by the particles *oc*, *oïl*, *sì*. To this extent, then, the Romance languages appear undifferentiated. It may also be worth pointing out that the notion of the 'ydioma tripharium' in no sense corresponds to the one expressed by the term Vulgar Latin (let alone Classical Latin). The notion is much more unitary than the modern one and it is also more closely associated with that of an ethnic group. One language–one people is an equation that is at the basis of much of Dante's thinking, in spite of the non-ethnic basis of the Babelic confusion of languages. On the other hand, it may be seen that Dante

* 'of that fair land where sounds the *sì*.'

had a clear conception of the genealogical or family-tree view of the origin and genesis of languages, very similar to the one current among nineteenth-century linguists, though of course it does not take account of phonetic evolution. The proof of a common origin of the Romance vernaculars is the fact that they have so many words in common; among these, Dante singles out the following in Latin: 'Deum', 'celum', 'amorem', 'mare', 'terram', 'est', 'vivit', 'moritur', 'amat' (*DVE*, I, viii, 6).

We have now reached a point in our exposition where an account of Dante's conception of the nature of Latin can no longer be delayed. For Dante, as for most medieval scholars, the nature of Latin is intimately bound up with the notion of *grammatica*. The two terms are very often synonymous. *Grammatica* stands for an orderly, in-corruptible, literary language fashioned by the art of man (hence the notion of artifact) to repair the impermanence and variability of the 'natural' vernaculars and thus permit communication across time and nations. The basis of *grammatica* is one or more vernaculars, and many *grammaticae* are therefore possible: Dante mentions Greek as well as Latin (*DVE*, I, i, 3). Latin could not, therefore, be the 'parent' of a vernacular: it is rather the other way round. Which vernacular or group of vernaculars did give rise to Latin in Dante's mind is not explicitly stated; presumably the vernacular of ancient Rome.

The basic opposition then between the two terms of the distinction is that of *artificialis* for the *grammaticae* and of *naturalis* for the vernaculars. In the *Convivio*, Latin is described as being superior to the vernacular on three counts: *nobilità*, since Latin is perpetual and incorruptible; *vertù*, since Latin is able to express a larger number of concepts than the vernacular; *bellezza*, since 'lo volgare seguita uso e lo latino arte'—the vernacular follows usage whereas Latin follows art (*Con*. i, v, 7–15). In the *De Vulgari Eloquentia*, on the other hand, it is the vernacular that is said to be the nobler of the two. This is partly because it was the first to have been used by mankind, partly because it is found the whole world over—though differentiated into many *prolationes* and *vocabula*, and partly because it is natural to us whereas Latin is artificial (*DVE*, i, i, 4). The change of mind could not be more complete.

One may be tempted to think that in writing the *De Vulgari Eloquentia* Dante was attempting to elevate the vernacular of Italy to the status and position of a *grammatica*. But this is not so. The two are on entirely different planes, the one natural, the other artificial. And in fact there are no precepts of an 'artificial' nature to be found in the work. Dante did elevate the vernacular to the position of a *grammatica*; but this was achieved by writing not the *De Vulgari Eloquentia* but the *Commedia*.

I have brought in, surreptitiously, a phrase I had not used before: 'the vernacular of Italy'. Till then, I had only talked of the vernaculars of Italy. In much the same way, almost surreptitiously—although the notion underlies the thinking behind the whole of the *De Vulgari*—Dante introduces in the second half of book i the concept of a refined type of vernacular, common to the whole of Italy, the *vulgaris illustris*.

The *volgare illustre*, to give the expression its more

familiar Italian form, is conceived by Dante as 'the vernacular of Italy' in the sense that the nobler parts of all the vernaculars of Italy are common to the whole country and may be considered as a distinct, ideal language, seen in its purest form in the writings of the best poets of the land. This nobility of language Dante finds in greater or lesser measure in all the municipal vernaculars of Italy, and yet it belongs exclusively to none. To this extent, then, the *volgare illustre* is a kind of abstraction, a linguistic ideal.

The qualities that go to make up the nobility of the *volgare illustre* are described to us by means of four adjectives: *illustris*, illustrious, for it throws light on those who use it and is itself illuminated by its users; *cardinalis*, pivotal, since all other Italian vernaculars revolve round it; *aulicus*, courtly, for if Italy had a royal court it would be used there; *curialis*, authoritative, for if the best minds in the country were united in a *curia*, again it would be used there.

It will be seen that at least three different criteria are used by Dante in defining the *volgare illustre*. First, there is a social criterion, political and intellectual in character, and reflected by the use of the adjectives *aulicus* and *curialis*; these two adjectives may be contrasted with *mediastinus* (*DVE*, I, xi, 6) or *mediocris* (*DVE*, I, xii, 6) used to describe persons of middle condition, and *montaninus* or *rusticanus* (*DVE*, I, xi, 6) used to describe the rustic vernaculars. Secondly, there is an aesthetic criterion, literary or stylistic in character, reflected in the use of *illustris* and perhaps also *cardinalis* if the word is understood to apply to a linguistic model. It is in fact mainly the language of poets in the vernacular that concerns Dante. In a later passage of the *De Vulgari*

(II, iv, 6), the *volgare illustre* is associated with the higher style and contrasted with two other types of *volgari*, *mediocris* and *humilis*, for the lower styles. Stylistic considerations play a crucial part not only in Dante's conception of the *volgare illustre* but also in that of other vernaculars. The *langue d'oïl*, for example, is thought to be particularly suitable to narrative genres and the *langue d'oc* to lyric poetry (*DVE*, I, x, 2–4).

Finally, there is a geographical criterion, but this time in a negative sense, in so far as the *volgare illustre* is not to be identified with any local vernacular; in this sense *cardinalis* is perhaps to be opposed to *municipalis*, applied to the local vernaculars.

With this geographical criterion in mind, Dante anticipates some possible objections from a parochially minded reader. And to forestall such opposition, before even embarking upon a full definition of the *volgare illustre*, Dante takes us on a grand review of the major Italian dialects, fourteen in number, enumerating and classifying them according to region, and describing them, though to a minimal extent (*DVE*, I, x–xv). One by one they are taken up only to be rejected, some summarily, others after a more impartial examination. These chapters are justly famous for their verve and raciness. The judgements are made on aesthetic grounds, assessing the relative beauty of words and of the sounds they contain. They range from a summary dismissal of Roman—not a vernacular, but a *tristiloquium*—to high praise of Bolognese—though it too is rejected on the grounds that Bologna's own major poets departed from their native vernacular. Tuscan is rejected in all its forms as a *turpiloquium*, although four Tuscan writers, including himself, do pass muster.

We now know that the language Dante admired and the one he himself used was in fact basically Tuscan, Florentine to be precise. It was a Florentine which had accepted many regional forms, particularly southern ones, and it contained a substantial number of latinisms and also gallicisms, both from north and south France. Nevertheless, it could not be described as anything but Tuscan. Dante was certainly under the impression that the best 'Sicilian' poets wrote in the *volgare illustre* (*DVE*, I, xii, 6): what he could not realize, and this misconception was to remain with us until the present century, was that the form in which the poems of the Sicilian school reached him had been given a thoroughly Tuscan look on being copied and circulated in Tuscany.

There is a sense in which the attribute *cardinalis* could be most appropriately applied to Tuscan when compared to the remaining dialects of Italy. Tuscany is centrally placed in the peninsula, mid-way between north and south, and linguistically Tuscan does reflect this position: it was in fact able to provide a kind of common denominator which proved acceptable to both north and south. Tuscan was also the most archaic of the Italian peninsular dialects and therefore closer to Latin, so that on the time axis too, as well as on the spatial one, it could be said to be more 'common' than any of the other two main groups.

We see, then, that for a variety of reasons Dante was misled as to the true nature of the language he used. We should not forget, however, that his quest was basically one for the language suitable for the highest style and that therefore it had to take place upon at least two planes at once. Popular Tuscan he could not accept: it was too municipal, too idiosyncratic to be identified with a literary language which had already had a considerable history in an almost national sense.

In a recent essay, Antonino Pagliaro has attempted a definition of Dante's salient contribution to the history of linguistics.[1] I can do no better than conclude by reporting his findings. These stress the fact that Dante developed clearly, perhaps more clearly than other writers before him, three major notions concerned with the dynamics of linguistic evolution: first, that linguistic forms evolve in relation to changes affecting man, both as an individual and in society; secondly, that a linguistic community may embrace a variety of dialects and local vernaculars; finally, that a common language may come into being as the result of a conscious process of election.

It is fashionable today to give high praise to the modernity of Dante's views regarding the nature of language and the linguistic state of the peninsula. I hope I have shown that much of this praise is justified.

[1] *Op. cit.* p. 215.

7

DANTE AND
THE ENGLISH POETS

C. P. BRAND

The essays which have preceded this one have summed up and re-interpreted aspects of Dante's thought and art. Their point of departure has been the text of Dante's writings, their aim to indicate what Dante means today, seven hundred years after his birth. The aim of this paper is different—it is to show what Dante has meant in the past to different generations of English readers and in particular to a number of English poets to whom Dante's example was significant and fruitful. My point of departure is the work of the English poets and critics, and I should not dare to enter this dark wood without the guidance of my 'maestro e autore', Paget Toynbee, whose vast anthology, *Dante in English Literature*, appeared more than fifty years ago and is still an indispensable guide to the English Dantista.[1] With the help of Toynbee and of a few later scholars, Friederich, Dédéyan and others, this paper will attempt not to repeat these scholars' findings and methods in a chronological survey of the English poets who studied and learned from Dante, but to draw certain broad conclusions from the material they have provided. The

[1] See P. Toynbee, *Dante in English Literature* (1909); W. P. Friederich, *Dante's Fame Abroad* (Rome, 1950); C. Dédéyan, *Dante en Angleterre* (Paris, 1964); O. Kuhns, *Dante and the English Poets* (1904).

question to answer here is how Dante has been interpreted and represented in England, and what aspects of his genius have made the greatest impression in this country. In a broad survey of this kind, which I do not think has been attempted before, I hope that the intention and the occasion will justify my summary treatment of so many great names.

Perhaps the most obvious concept of Dante that occurs to the English reader is that of Dante the patriot, the man who was deeply involved in the political turmoils of his age, who spoke out fearlessly against pettiness and corruption and suffered exile for his beliefs. This is essentially, in England as in Italy, a nineteenth-century view. It was the view of men who were themselves involved in a great political upheaval in the Napoleonic Wars and the subsequent struggle for freedom and independence in Italy, and of those who supported them. It was a view spread in England by a small band of Italian political exiles of the first decades of the nineteenth century who came to this country to escape persecution at home and who were able to make a living teaching Italian and writing for English journals—Foscolo, Rossetti, Berchet, Panizzi, Mazzini and others. To these men Dante was their great forerunner in exile, the first great Italian patriot.[1] Mazzini, writing in the *Westminster Review* in 1837, pointed to Foscolo, much of whose critical work first appeared in this country, as the leader in a new trend of Dante studies:

Foscolo was perhaps the first who undertook the study and

[1] For Dante in early nineteenth-century England see C. P. Brand, *Italy and the English Romantics* (Cambridge, 1957), ch. IV.

the culture of Dante as of a profound patriot. He recognised
in Dante more than the poet,—more than the creator of
language; he recognised in him the great citizen, the reformer,
the poet of the religion, the prophet of the nationality of
Italy.

This was the view that was impressed by the Italian exiles
on the English poets of their time: Byron, Shelley,
Sotheby, Hunt, Hemans, Rogers. Wordsworth's musings
before the *Sasso di Dante* by the *Duomo* in Florence are
revealing:

> As a true man, who long had served the lyre,
> I gazed with earnestness, and dared no more.
> But in his breast the mighty Poet bore
> A Patriot's heart, warm with undying fire.
> Bold with the thought, in reverence I sate down,
> And, for a moment, filled that empty Throne.

This too was Byron's view: 'I don't wonder at the enthusiasm of the Italians about Dante. He is the poet of liberty.
Persecution, exile, the dread of a foreign grave, could not
shake his principles.' Byron's *Prophecy of Dante* was inspired by his picture of Dante the outcast, Byron's own
precursor in exile:

> To live in narrow ways with little men,
> A common sight to every common eye,
> A wanderer, while even wolves can find a den,
> Ripp'd from all kindred, from all home, all things
> That make communion sweet, and soften pain—
> To feel me in the solitude of kings
> Without the power that makes them bear a crown—
> To envy every dove his nest and wings.

(I, 161–8.)

Byron like Dante was afraid that he would 'leave his bones in a strange land', and he puts into Dante's mouth his own impassioned plea that the Italians should unite and 'make the Alps impassable' (II, 145)—this in spite of the fact that Dante called for a German Emperor to come to Italy to put an end to the factions of his age, and that his concept of universal peace was based on imperial authority, that it was supra-national.

It was this concept of the exile, the great patriot rejected by his own contemporaries, which inspired numerous apostrophes to Dante in the nineteenth century. Perhaps the best example after Byron's poem is Dante Gabriel Rossetti's *Dante at Verona*. Rossetti was himself the son of an exile of the 1820's and a famous Dante scholar, and his poem is perhaps a filial tribute to the old man who maintained his principles through all his misfortunes. He imagines Dante refusing a pardon from the Florentines:

> This Dante writ in answer thus
> . . . .
> That since no gate led by God's will
> To Florence, but the one whereat
> The priests and money-changers sat,
> He still would wander; for that still
> Even through the body's prison-bars,
> His soul possessed the sun and stars.

Wider than this concept of the poet-patriot-exile was that of Dante the bard, the singer who summed up the culture and thought of his age and who gave expression to its still only half-understood and half-realized aspirations. Again it was the nineteenth-century critics and poets who emphasized this view, who analysed literature as part of a historical process and tried to bring the writers of their own age into a closer relationship with the social, political and philosophical currents of the time. In the debates on the function of the poet, Dante's great example was frequently cited in England, by Foscolo above all, and then by Hazlitt, Macaulay, Coleridge and Shelley. Coleridge in his lecture on Dante declared that 'Dante was himself eminently a picture of the age in which he lived; [...] he was the living link between religion and philosophy; he philosophized the religion and christianized the philosophy of Italy.' His great achievement was 'a combination of poetry with doctrine'.[1] This approach to Dante was particularly significant for Shelley, who probably knew Dante's works better than any other of the Romantic poets. Dante is a keystone in Shelley's *Defence of Poetry*: he was

the second poet (after Homer) the series of whose creations bore a defined and intelligible relation to the knowledge and sentiment and religion of the age in which he lived and of the ages which followed it [...] Dante was the first religious reformer, [...] and the first awakener of entranced Europe; he created a language in itself music and persuasion, out of a chaos of inharmonious barbarisms.

This view of Dante as the combined poet, philosopher and politician, the man of action whose poetry was the extension and adjunct of his political career, has, I think, entered the minds of many poets and critics. Perhaps the most interesting off-shoot in English poetry is Browning's

[1]   S. T. Coleridge, *Literary Remains*, 1836, I, 154.

Sordello. *Sordello* is essentially the story of the medieval poet, forerunner of Dante, who, by contrast with Dante, failed to fulfil his very high poetic ambitions. He is presented by Browning as a study of a poet questing for his soul through his activities as soldier, lover and champion of the masses. He is the great visionary who fails, for reasons of temperament, precisely where Dante succeeded. Browning's Italian teacher, Angelo Cerutti, had recently published in England Daniello Bartoli's *De' Simboli Trasportati al Morale* (1830), and Browning was led to the *Purgatorio* by Bartoli's comments on Sordello and Dante. Dante tells us little of Sordello except by presenting him as a patriot and stern critic of the princes in Canto VII, and Browning decided to use Sordello as a sort of therapeutic exploration of the poet's mission:[1] he will show another side of Sordello to that revealed in Dante:

> ...for he is Thine!
> Sordello, thy fore-runner, Florentine.
> . . . .
> Still, what if I approach the august sphere
> Named now with only one name, disentwine
> That undercurrent soft and argentine
> From its fierce mate in the majestic mass
> Leavened as the sea whose fire was mixt with glass
> In John's transcendent vision—launch once more
> That lustre? Dante, pacer of the shore
> Where glutted hell disgorgeth filthiest gloom,
> Unbitten by its whirring sulphur-spume....
>
> (Book I, ll. 347–68.)

Browning struggled for years with this difficult subject, his

[1] See R. Griffin, *Life of Browning* (1910), ch. VI.

problems increased by the intrusion of a Mrs W. Busk who brought out her poem, *Sordello*, in the meantime. If Browning 'disentwined' Sordello from Dante, Mrs Busk clutched him to her romantic heart:

> Come listen to the tale I tell
> Of him who sang, who lov'd so well,
> The Mantuan Troubadour, renown'd Sordel.[1]

Not many Italian heroes escaped the Mrs Busks of the nineteenth century.

The concept of the poet-philosopher did not appeal to all. Dante's preoccupation with difficult philosophical and theological problems has been a stumbling block to many English readers, to Byron, for example, who complained that 'the *Divine Comedy* is a scientific treatise of some theological student.... The poem is so obscure, tiresome and insupportable that no-one can read it for half an hour together without yawning and going to sleep over it.'[2] For many others however Dante's religious views were of great interest. From at least the sixteenth century Dante was seen as the outspoken critic of the corruption of the Church of Rome, an ally of the Protestant cause from within the Catholic camp. Fynes Moryson declared in 1594: 'Surely Petrarch, Dantes and other free wits of Italy did see the Papall frauds before the Germanes, and though fearefully, yet plainly, pronounced Rome to be Babylon'[3]—and John Foxe in his *Book of Martyrs* (1570) held up Dante as an opponent of the Papacy.

---

[1] Mrs W. Busk, *Plays and Poems* (1837), II, 1.
[2] T. Medwin, *Life of Shelley* (1847), II, 252–3.
[3] See C. Hughes, *Shakespeare's Europe* (1903), III, 41.

It is in this role that Milton most often speaks of Dante.
In *Of Reformation touching Church Discipline* he translates
three lines from *Inf.* XIX:

> Ah Constantine! of how much ill was cause,
>> Not thy Conversion, but those rich demaines
>> That the first wealthy pope receiv'd of thee;[1]

and in *Lycidas* he echoes two lines from the *Paradiso* con-
demning false priests. Most critics have recognized that
it was a fundamental kinship of temperament that led
Milton to his eager study of Dante: 'possum tamen non-
nunquam ad illum Dantem, et Petrarcham [. . .] libenter et
cupide commessatum ire'*.[2] Milton's opposition to Arch-
bishop Laud is paralleled by Dante's to Boniface; Milton's
disappointment at Cromwell's death by Dante's at the
death of Henry VII. That Milton was stimulated and sustained by Dante's example in writing an epic on the moral
condition of mankind I do not think can be denied. Milton's
treatment is of course totally independent of the *Comedy*
but generations of English readers have seen the parallel—
Richardson, Cary, Coleridge, Hunt, Hazlitt, Macaulay.
Perhaps Herford has put this view most succinctly:

The *Divine Comedy* is the story of how Dante, baffled by the
failure of the State to govern and of the Church to guide, was
shown by Virgil 'another way' to the lost Paradise of earthly
happiness, and finally by Beatrice to the heaven of eternal
welfare. Its aim, as Dante tells us, was to show how men at
large might thus escape from misery in this life and win happiness thereafter. . . . And Milton's *Paradise Lost*, in its final effect

---

[1] J. Milton, *Prose Works* (1953), I, 558; cf. *Inf.* XIX, 115–17.

[2] Letter to Buonmattei, Sept. 1638 (Familiar Letter VIII).

* 'I can however sometimes return willingly and eagerly to delight
in the company of Dante and Petrarch.'

if not in original intention, is an intimation also to the ruined army of Puritanism, that there was another way which the individual soul could traverse by its own insight and resolution alone.[1]

Milton has one other significant reference to Dante which we have not mentioned. In his *Apology for Smectymnuus* he wrote: 'Above them all (I) preferred the two famous renowners of Beatrice and Laura, who never write but honour of them to whom they devote their verse, displaying sublime and pure thoughts, without transgression.'[2] Milton's respect for the purity of Dante's love for Beatrice has provoked interesting parallels between the relationship of *Comus* to *Paradise Lost* and of the *Vita Nuova* to the *Divina Commedia*, which we can hardly pursue here. But Milton's view of Dante as the 'renowner of Beatrice' has of course been one of the most persistent and fruitful readings of Dante's work. Dante's place in the long Platonic tradition of love has been recognized by many English poets. To them, as for example to Shelley, he represented that development in the Platonic tradition by which a woman was interposed as the medium between man and the divinity, and man's ideal love for woman was conceived as a purifying and ennobling influence raising him to the divine love. Dante's supreme achievement was his expression of the ideal love after which Shelley strove, his 'seeking in a mortal image the likeness of what is perhaps eternal'. This is his view in *The Triumph of Life*, where Dante is the man who:

[1] C. H. Herford, 'Dante and Milton', *Bulletin of John Rylands Library*, VIII (Manchester, 1924), 228.
[2] J. Milton, *Prose Works* (1953), I, 890.

> . . . from the lowest depths of hell,
> Through every paradise and through all glory,
> Love led serene, and who returned to tell
> In words of hate and awe, the wondrous story
> How all things are transfigured except Love.
>
> (ll. 472–6.)

This Dantesque conception of a universe animated by love underlies *Prometheus Unbound* and certainly contributed to *Epipsychidion*, which is prefaced by an almost literal translation from Dante's *Canzone* 'Voi ch'intendendo il terzo ciel movete', and an explicit parallel with Dante's *Vita Nuova*. The 'spiritual union of the soul and the thing loved', of which Dante wrote in *Convivio* (in a passage which Shelley copied out) is fundamental to Shelley's poem—a union not analysed with Dante's precision but 'felt' with a compelling force.[1]

Dante is of course only one strand in the complex web of Shelley's Platonism, but Shelley's appreciation of the broad significance of Dante's love led the way to a wider reading of Dante in England. Whereas most late eighteenth-century readers knew only the *Inferno*, Shelley emphasized the beauties of the other *cantiche*, and also drew attention to the *Vita Nuova*. In the pursuit of Dante's love for Beatrice a number of scholars and poets now turned to Dante's lyric poetry—Arthur Hallam, for example, Tennyson's friend, who made versions from Dante's sonnets, and Dante Gabriel Rossetti, who translated the whole of the *Vita Nuova*, and whose original verse often reproduces the idiom of his translation. Yet the gap between Rossetti and

---

[1] See N. Rogers, *Shelley at Work* (Oxford, 1956), p. 236.

Dante is great. Dante's love for Beatrice, thoughtfully and patiently analysed and explained in the *Vita Nuova* in its relation to the love of God, consciously subordinated and integrated in a higher purpose in the *Comedy*, is remote from Rossetti's romantic love, which is its own end. Rossetti's translation, closely as it follows the text, slurs over Dante's precise philosophical terms because he does not fully understand or sympathize with them, and the *House of Life* sonnets and *The Blessed Damozel* (which Eliot later complained came between him and Dante) are remote in spirit, as in style, from Dante's love poetry:

> There will I ask of Christ the Lord
> Thus much for him and me:—
> Only to live as once on earth
> With Love—only to be
> As then awhile for ever now
> Together, I and he.[1]

And remote too are Christina Rossetti's *Monna Innominata* sonnets which spring from her dissatisfaction with Beatrice, 'resplendent with charms but...scant of attractiveness'.[2]

Browning too shared this interest in Dante's lyric poetry. His sequence of love poems for his wife, *One Word More*, is an offering such as Dante made to Beatrice when he drew an angel for her (as he tells us in the *Vita Nuova*) and was interrupted by 'certain people of importance' (later the title of another group of Browning's poems). It was

[1] See 'The Blessed Damozel'. See also Nicolette Gray, *Rossetti, Dante and Ourselves* (1947).
[2] See C. Rossetti's Preface to the *Monna Innominata* sonnets.

Dante the lover who appealed to the Brownings, not the grim Dante of the *Inferno*:

> You and I would rather see that angel
> Painted by the tenderness of Dante,
> Would we not? than read a fresh *Inferno*.   (VI.)

—and Browning later wrote into Elizabeth's Testament a version of Dante's words from the *Convivio*: 'Thus I believe, thus I affirm, thus I am certain it is, that from this life I shall pass to another, better, where that lady lives of whom my soul was enamoured.'[1]

Browning's resistance to a 'fresh *Inferno*' is typical of a large group of English readers for whom Dante was too grim, melancholic, unrelenting, severe, embittered by his unhappy experiences in exile.[2] 'Grim Dante pressed his lips' was Tennyson's image; and Macaulay: 'In every line of the *Divine Comedy* we discern the asperity which is produced by pride struggling with misery'; and Landor: 'I find the features of Ugolino reflected full in Dante. The two characters are similar in themselves, hard, cruel, inflexible, malignant'; and Leigh Hunt: 'The swarthy Florentine had not the healthy temperament of his brethren and he fell upon evil times. Compared with Homer and Shakespeare his very intensity seems only superior to theirs from an excess of the morbid.... He wanted the music of a happy and a happy-making disposition.' Many tales were current of Dante's biting tongue. Sir John

---

[1] Cf. *Con*. II, vii, 16.

[2] See A. Tennyson, 'Palace of Art'; T. B. Macaulay, 'Essay on Milton', *Edinburgh Review* (Aug. 1825); W. S. Landor, *Pentameron* (*Complete Works*, 1927, IX, 164); L. Hunt, *Stories from the Italian Poets* (1907), p. 48.

Harington in his *Most Elegant and Wittie Epigrams* (1615) reported one:

> *A good answer of the Poet Dant to an Atheist.*
> The pleasant learn'd Italian Poet Dant,
> Hearing an Atheist at the Scriptures jest:
> Askt him in jest, which was the greatest beast?
> He simply said; he thought an Elephant.
> Then Elephant (quoth Dant) it were commodious
> That thou wouldst hold thy peace, or get thee hence,
> Breeding our Conscience scandall and offence
> With thy profaned speech, most vile and odious.
>   Oh Italy, thou breed'st but few such Dants,
>   I would our England bred no Elephants.   (IV, 17.)

This haughty intolerant personality is reflected in the *Comedy* in a harsh, incisive, often abrupt and severe style which only rarely recurs in Dante's translators, imitators and followers. Chaucer writes often with Dante in mind, but his tone is so much lighter. Compare for example Dante's grim warning over the gates of Hell:

> Per me si va ne la città dolente,
>   per me si va ne l'etterno dolore...*   (*Inf.* III, 1–2.)

with Chaucer's inscription over the gates to the garden in *The Parlement of Foules*:

> Thorgh me men gon into that blysful place...
> Be glad, thow redere, and thy sorwe of-caste;
> Al open am I—passe in, and sped thee faste! (ll. 127–33.)

The differences of temperament between Chaucer and Dante stand out, too, in *The House of Fame*. Dante in the

---

* 'Through me is the way into the woeful city, through me is the way to everlasting pain.'

Purgatorio, carried up above the earth by an eagle, retains his pride and dignity—and his reaction in *Paradiso* is one of haughty scorn for the pettiness of the earth:

> Col viso ritornai per tutte quante
>   le sette spere, e vidi questo globo
>   tal, ch'io sorrisi del suo vil sembiante.★
>
> (Par. XXII, 133–5.)

Chaucer makes fun of himself on the eagle's back:

> Me caryinge in his clawes starke
> As lyghtly as I were a larke...   (ll. 545–6.)

and when he looks down at the earth he is only impressed in his naïve way with the extent of the view and how small everything appears:

> Now ryveres, now citees,
> Now tounes, and now grete trees,
> Now shippes seyllynge in the see.
>   But thus sone in a while he
>   Was flowen fro the ground so hye
>   That al the world, as to myn yë,
>   No more semed than a prikke.   (ll. 901–7.)[1]

A similar passage occurs in Sir David Lyndsay's *The Dreme* (1528), a visionary journey through hell, purgatory and highest heaven with a good deal of social criticism, but quite lacking Dante's venom and urgency of purpose.[2] Even Dante's admirers found it hard to understand his spleen.

[1] See C. Looten, 'Chaucer et Dante', *Revue de Littérature Comparée*, v (1925).

[2] See ll. 610–28.

★ 'With my gaze I returned through all the seven spheres, and I saw this globe such that I smiled at its mean appearance.'

Dante and the English Poets

We have so far examined differing aspects of Dante's personality as viewed by his English readers—Dante the patriot, Dante the bard, Dante the reformer, Dante the lover, Dante the hater. But what of Dante's art, of Dante the poet? Has Dante's poetry been understood and appreciated as poetry, and has his example been of significance to the English poets? This is a far more difficult question to answer, and it will be necessary to make far more reservations and qualifications than hitherto. The first and most obvious impediment to the diffusion of Dante's poetry in this country has been its obscurity. Ever since the sixteenth century English readers have commented on the difficulty of understanding Dante: 'Boccace is prettie hard, yet understood; Petrarche harder, but explained; Dante hardest but commented. Some doubt if all aright,' wrote Florio in his *World of Wordes*.[1] 'Dante is hard and few can understand him,' wrote Ben Jonson in *Volpone*.[2] Thomas Rymer complained in 1674 that 'the thoughts of Dante are so profound that much art is required to dive into them. Poetry demands a more clear air, and what is less incomprehensible.'[3] The Earl of Chesterfield tried in vain to read Dante and concluded that Dante did not think clearly: 'Though I formerly knew Italian extremely well I could never understand him; for which reason I had done with him, fully convinced that he was not worth the pains necessary to understand him.'[4] Of those who did read Dante's poem relatively few got

[1] *Epistle Dedicatorie.*
[2] Act III, sc. 2.
[3] T. Rymer, *Reflections on Aristotle's Treatise* (1674), p. 42.
[4] P. D. Stanhope, *Letters* (1892), I, 320.

beyond the *Inferno*, at least in the century from 1750–1850
—and not until the latter half of the nineteenth century was
Dante's lyric poetry at all well known.

Perhaps because of its obscurity translators of the *Comedy*
were slow to come forward. Not until 1782 was the first
complete translation of the *Inferno* published, and not until
1802 did the first translation of the whole *Comedy* appear.[1]
Since that date there have been numerous versions, both
of the entire poem and of parts of it, but many of these have
been little better than paraphrases. The difficulties of translating Dante into English verse are enormous and I can
only hint at the problems here. Dante's *terza rima* has been
the main stumbling block—it is an important vehicle for
his narrative style and the substitutes used by English
translators have nearly always proved inadequate—heroic
couplets, blank verse, six-line stanzas. Not until 1842 was
a whole *cantica* translated in the original metre; since then
many translators have opted for *terza rima*, and there have
been several brave attempts. Apart from the difficulty of
approximating to the length of Dante's tercets, the con-
tinual problem of finding three rhymes in English (relatively easy in an inflected language like Italian) forces the
translator frequently into paraphrase or padding, and the
injustice to Dante, who rarely uses a superfluous word, is
striking. Before the nineteenth century if one did not
know Italian one could read Dante in Grangier's heavy and
clumsy French translation, published in 1596, or in Serra-
valle's Latin version of 1417, but these were very dim
reflexions of Dante—and the samples translated by those

[1] By C. Rogers and H. Boyd, respectively.

who knew Italian, such as William Barker in his version (1568) of Gelli's *Capricci*, were often very misleading—incorrect versions of misprinted quotations with optimistic commentaries. Even Rossetti in the early nineteenth century could devise a crack-brained interpretation of the *Comedy* as an instrument in an international plot to overthrow the Church of Rome, and get an English publisher to print it and an English miss to translate it.[1]

Yet more than one English poet of note has sharpened his wits translating Dante. Milton tried a few lines, and Gray attempted the Ugolino episode. Shelley translated some of Dante's lyric poetry and also fifty lines from the *Purgatorio* in the original metre. Of the full-length translations only one has achieved the distinction of being considered as poetry in its own right, but that, like Harington's *Orlando Furioso* and Fairfax's *Jerusalem Delivered*, has become a minor English classic. The Rev. H. F. Cary's translation, (printed 1805–14), was commended by Coleridge at a course of lectures in London in 1818, and it soon became famous. A second edition came out in 1819 and a third and fourth in 1831 and 1844. Its influence on contemporary poets was remarkable.[2] Whether or not Coleridge's first close acquaintance with the *Comedy* dates from his meeting with Cary, his first serious critical appreciation of the poem does not occur until the following year. Wordsworth thought Cary's translation 'a great national work', and Keats, who did not know Italian, took

[1] See E. R. Vincent, *G. Rossetti in England*, Oxford, 1936.
[2] See R. W. King, *The Translator of Dante* (1925). Toynbee, *op. cit.* I, 466, 541, 605, 617; II, 244, 385.

'those three little volumes' as his only reading on his Scottish tour in 1818. Shelley, who came to know Dante intimately, first studied the original by the aid of Cary, while Southey thought the translation 'very meritorious'. Lamb called it a 'polar-star translation', and Rogers claimed to have introduced it to Wordsworth. Coleridge thought that Cary's blank verse was 'the most varied and harmonious to my ear of any since Milton'.

Thus for many early nineteenth-century English readers Dante meant Cary, and the Italian text was not well known. Dante's poetry was shirked by many and mis-understood by many others because it *is* difficult. Others it has repelled because it is too 'crude'. Dante's habit of calling a spade a spade, his occasional use of vulgar language to describe obscene gestures and actions, his presentation of scenes of grim and even revolting realism, have offended many English readers. Coleridge spoke of Dante's 'occasional fault of becoming grotesque from being too graphic without imagination;...many of his images excite bodily disgust and not moral fear'.[1] Too many readers judged Dante on the *Inferno* and never came to know the delicacy and tenderness of the *Paradiso* or the lyric poetry. 'Such broiling, gashing, freezing and whirling', wrote Anna Seward, the Swan of Lichfield, in 1805; 'the terrible graces of the *Inferno* lose all their dignity in butcherly, grid-iron, and intestinal exhibitions.'[2] Landor in an Imaginary Conversation has Petrarch declare, 'The filthiness of some passages would disgrace the drunkenest

---

[1] S. T. Coleridge, *Literary Remains* (1836), I, 166.
[2] A. Seward, *Letters* (1811), VI, 225.

horse-dealer,' to which Boccaccio adds, 'Admirable is indeed the description of Ugolino to whoever can endure the sight of an old soldier gnawing at the scalp of an old arch-bishop'.[1] The *Gentleman's Magazine*, in reviewing Cary's translation, quoted Cary's statement that Dante was one of the most obscure writers, but by an inspired misprint substituted 'obscene' for 'obscure'.[2] Dante's so-called obscenity was at times much exaggerated by readers even in Italy. Phrases quite innocent in their context were lifted from the text and misinterpreted: some of these became so widely known that their original meaning was quite forgotten. Italian Cinquecento writers particularly condemned Dante for his 'basso stile'. Giovanni della Casa, in his treatise on manners, gave a wide currency to some of these phrases: we should avoid using words, he said, that are 'unhonest, foule and filthie, as some men say these are of Dant'. Robert Peterson, in his English translation of the *Galateo* (1576), repeats these criticisms, many of which are quite off the mark—a vulgar gesture made by Vanni Fucci is here attributed to a woman and followed up by: 'But *our* women would be much ashamed to speak so.'[3]

Relatively few English readers, however, have fully appreciated the savour of Dante's language or his linguistic theories. Dryden has several allusions to Dante's influence on the Italian vernacular:

> ...Dante's polish'd page
> Restor'd a silver, not a golden age.[4]

[1] W. S. Landor, *Complete Works* (1928), IX, 154, 164.

[2] June 1805, LXXV, 551.

[3] Fos. 81 *et seq.*   [4] J. Dryden, *Poems* (1958), I, 387.

But the more significant comments occur in the Romantic period when Dante was seen as a forerunner in the attempt to create a common language. Coleridge for example was able on several occasions to point to the *De Vulgari Eloquentia* in support of his theories of poetic diction. The attempt of Coleridge and Wordsworth to bring their poetic diction closer to the spoken language as opposed to a traditional literary dialect was a recurrence to the same principles which guided Dante in the *Comedy* and Chaucer. But Wordsworth's preoccupation with the 'real' language of men in 'low and rustic life' was criticized by Coleridge: 'the *lingua communis*...is no more to be found in the phraseology of low and rustic life than in that of any other class....Anterior to cultivation the *lingua communis* of every country, as Dante has well observed, exists everywhere in parts and nowhere as a whole'; and elsewhere Coleridge reverts to Dante's theory of a 'cardinal, courtly and curial' vulgar tongue purged of local peculiarities.[1]

Dante's views on language and his linguistic practice have been particularly significant for a number of twentieth-century English poets, Eliot and Pound in particular, who have understood and respected Dante's achievement as a 'preserver and enricher' of Italian.[2] Eliot on several occasions refers to Dante's concern for 'real, living and powerful language'; his work was 'the perfection of common language'. The influence of Dante's bold choice of words, his directness, on the formation of Eliot's

[1] S. T. Coleridge, *Biographia Literaria* (1907), II, 41; *Anima Poetae*, (1895), 229–30.

[2] See T. S. Eliot's *Selected Essays* (1951), p. 252; E. Pound, *Literary Essays* (1954), p. 205; and his *Letters* (1951), pp. 349, 378.

precise, concise, often conversational style must have been considerable. Pound contributed to Eliot's views here: 'The border-line between "gee-whiz" and Milton's tumefied dialect must exist (Dante in *De Vulgari Eloquentia* seems to have thought of a good many particulars of the problem)', and Pound praised Binyon's translation of the *Inferno* precisely because he 'has got rid of pseudo-magniloquence, of puffed words. I don't remember a single decorative or rhetorical word in his first ten cantos.' The *De Vulgari Eloquentia*, he considered, was 'badly needed in a sloppy and slobbering world'.

An early nineteenth-century critic who noticed the linguistic parallel between Dante and the English Romantics went on as follows:

It may be a singular observation but we believe it to be a just one that the modern school of poetry which has arisen in this country within the last thirty years, comes closer to the manner of Dante than any other; and this very remarkable poet actually combines many of the leading traits of the most eminent of our distinguished contemporaries.

The early nineteenth-century poets were reminiscent of Dante in their close observation of nature, their long metaphysical and theological discussions, and 'their constant attempt to excite emotion by laying bare the blackest passions of the soul in all their naked enormity, and dwelling upon all the most wretched vices and afflictions of human nature'.[1] On the latter qualities in particular Dante's fame rested for many years. He was praised for 'the sterner and darker passions on which he delights to

[1] *Edinburgh Magazine* (Dec. 1818), III, 226.

dwell'; for his genius as a 'master of the terrible', as in the Ugolino story where he outdid the terror-novelists themselves. Macaulay in a famous parallel between Dante and Milton, which appeared in 1824, wrote as follows:

I will frankly confess that the vague sublimity of Milton affects me less than these reviled details of Dante. We read Milton and we know that we are reading a great poet. When we read Dante the poet vanishes. We are listening to the man who has returned from 'the valley of the dolorous abyss';—we seem to see the dilated eye of horror, to hear the shuddering accents with which he tells his fearful tale.[1]

Dante was widely praised too as the master of pathos. One of the best-known episodes was that of Pia de' Tolomei, who appears briefly in *Purg.* v, as the victim of her jealous husband who condemned her to die in the Tuscan marshes. Samuel Rogers referred to it in his *Italy*, and it was a favourite passage of Byron's. It inspired a lengthy poem by William Herbert published in 1820, and others by Mrs Hemans and Mrs Yorick Smythies in the 1830's. Tennyson's *Mariana in the South*, which appeared at about the same time, is on the same theme. It is Dante's very brevity which is so tempting:

> ricorditi di me che son la Pia:
> Siena mi fé; disfecemi Maremma;
> salsi colui che 'nnanellata pria
> disposando m'avea con la sua gemma.*

> (*Purg.* v, 133–6.)

[1] T. B. Macaulay, *Complete Works* (1898), xi, 267.

* 'Remember me who am Pia. Siena created me, Maremma destroyed me. He knows that who first plighted his troth and then wedded me with his gem.'

The English versions expand these hints into long poems, and in seeking pathos fall into melodrama or a pathetic sentimentality. Felicia Hemans introduces a child:

> Such pangs were thine, young mother! thou didst bend
> O'er thy fair boy and raise his drooping head.[1]

Mrs Smythies contrives an operatic aria for the doomed bride against a gloomy back-cloth:

> The snake's green scales seemed in the sun to glow,
> The wild wolf's eyes glared on them from the shade;
> No human form was seen.[2]

It is rare indeed that the English poets match Dante's pathos—witness the Ugolino episode, translated by Chaucer, Gray, Richard Wharton, Medwin with Shelley's help, Hallam, even Gladstone among others. Sir Joshua Reynolds's painting of Ugolino was very widely admired. Joseph Warton said of this passage, 'I cannot recollect any passage, in any writer whatever, so truly pathetic.'[3] Shelley observed that Byron studied it deeply and thought that he would never have written the *Prisoner of Chillon* without it.[4] Yet the essential greatness of Dante's lines constantly escapes his imitators—Chaucer, for example, in his version in the *Monk's Tale*. Dante introduces Ugolino as a sinner—he is a traitor and we first see him gnawing the skull of Archbishop Ruggieri:

> La bocca sollevò dal fiero pasto
> quel peccator....*   (*Inf.* XXXIII, 1–2.)

---

[1] F. Hemans, 'The Maremma', *Works* (1880), p. 279.

[2] H. M. Smythies, *The Bride of Siena* (1835), p. 67.

[3] J. Warton, *Essay on Pope* (1806), I, 252.

[4] T. Medwin, *Life of Shelley* (1847), II, 22.

* 'That sinner raised his mouth from his savage meal.'

The pathos is implicit in his situation—traitor or no, he is still a father. Chaucer advertises his intention:

> Ther may no tonge telle for pitee,

and he plays for our pity, exaggerating the helplessness of the children:

> The eldest scarsly fyf yeer was of age.

Ugolino's struggle to control his anguish before his children is lost by Chaucer. Dante's Ugolino does not weep or wail; he dies, sinner as he is, like a 'grande vinto', biting his hands in silent grief. Chaucer may call his Hugelyn 'the myghty Erl of Pize' but he reveals nothing of his might:

> 'Allas!' quod he, 'allas that I was wroght!'
> Therwith the teeris fillen from his yen.[1]

Others were fascinated by the horrific elements in the story. Ugolino's last words, 'poscia più che 'l dolor poté 'l digiuno' (*Inf.* xxxiii, 75) (literally, 'fasting was more powerful than grief') are normally taken to mean that Ugolino's suffering was brought to an end by his dying of starvation. But these ambiguous words, together with other grim hints in the text (Ugolino gnawing the Archbishop's skull, and biting his hands) gave rise to a legend, accepted by Byron, that Ugolino was driven by his hunger to feed on his children after they were dead. Shelley was shocked: 'The story is horrible enough without such a comment.'[2]

[1] See T. Spencer, 'The Story of Ugolino in Dante and Chaucer', *Speculum* (1934), ix, 295.
[2] T. Medwin, *Shelley* (1847), ii, 22. See F. D'Ovidio, 'Le ultime parole di Ugolino', *Ugolino, etc.* (Milan, 1907).

Chaucer's approach to Dante's theme, softening, diluting and explaining it, is characteristic of the interpretation Dante has most often received in England. The English treatment of Dante's themes is rarely so forthright, stark and unrelenting as in the original. Dante's Ulysses, for example, tells the story of the end of his great voyage, in his old age, inspired by a noble (but in Dante's view misplaced) urge to extend the frontiers of knowledge (only hints of which are in the classical sources). Tennyson's poem is on this same theme, a last great enterprise to crown an adventurous life—'there is an echo of Dante in it,' Tennyson said, and several passages echo the celebration of the human spirit which Dante puts in Ulysses' mouth:

> Considerate la vostra semenza:
> fatti non foste a viver come bruti,
> ma per seguir virtute e canoscenza.*
>
> (Inf. XXVI, 118–20.)

> ...and vile it were
> For some three suns to store and hoard myself
> And this gray spirit yearning in desire
> To follow knowledge like a sinking star
> Beyond the utmost bound of human thought.
>
> (ll. 28–32.)

But Dante's Ulysses, like Ugolino, is a sinner; he is imprisoned in a flame for fraud—to Leigh Hunt's horror: 'Why poor Ulysses should find himself in hell after his immersion and be condemned to a swathing of eternal fire, while St Dominic, who deluged Christianity with fire and blood, is called a cherubic light, the Papist, not the poet,

---

* 'Consider the seed from which you are born; you were not born to live like brutes, but to follow virtue and knowledge.'

must explain.'[1] This rejection of Dante's hard, dispassionate analysis of moral states we have already noted in Chaucer's version of Ugolino—and it recurs too in the English interpretations of Paolo and Francesca—Rossetti's water-colour, for example, idealizing the kiss which in Dante is overlaid by the 'miseria' of damnation. There is nothing of Ulysses' sin in Tennyson, but neither is there anything of his tragic end. Dante's Ulysses shows both the questing spirit of man and the defeat of his aspirations, and Dante lets him sink with his ship without a comment. Tennyson is optimistic, idealistic, didactic. He pictures only the beginning of this great enterprise and does not even hint at failure, and he drives his message home:

> ...that which we are we are:
> One equal temper of heroic hearts,
> Made weak by time and fate, but strong in will
> To strive, to seek, to find and not to yield.

> (ll. 67–70.)

Eliot on the other hand was attracted by the shipwreck, and if Pound had not persuaded him to cut it out he would have included a long passage on this in *The Waste Land*—the only trace now is the 'Death by Water' of the Phoenician sailor.

Another reaction to Dante's severity of theme and style has been not a toning down, but an exaggeration with humorous intent, or a sly mockery. The *Comedy* lends itself to parody—Lorenzo de' Medici's *I Beoni* is a good example. Some of Dante's grim scenes have provoked amusing English reactions, Ugolino in particular, on

[1] L. Hunt, *The Indicator* (1834), I, 90.

whom one poet punned with 'You-go-lean-o' and of
whom Byron wrote in *Don Juan*:

> And if Pedrillo's fate should shocking be,
> Remember Ugolino condescends
> To eat the head of his arch-enemy
> The moment after he politely ends
> His task: if foes be food in hell, at sea
> 'Tis surely fair to dine upon our friends
> When shipwreck's short allowance grows too scanty
> Without being much more horrible than Dante.
>
> (II, 83.)

Eliot, too, gains some fine ironic effects from Dante
reminiscences:

> Under the brown fog of a winter dawn
> A crowd flowed over London bridge, so many
> I had not thought death had undone so many.
> Sighs short and infrequent were exhaled.
>
> (*Waste Land*, 61–4; cf. *Inf.* III, 56.)

—and Dante's lines on Pia are parodied ('Siena mi fé,
disfecemi Maremma'):

> Highbury bore me. Richmond and Kew
> Undid me.   (*Waste Land*, 293–4.)

Chaucer's tone at times sounds like an extension of the
restrained humour of the *Comedy*: Virgil's chaffing Dante
reappears in the words of the Hoste to Chaucer in the
Prologue to Sir Thopas:

> And seyde thus, 'what man artow? quod he;
> 'Thou lookest as thou woldest fynde an hare,
> For evere upon the ground I se thee stare.'
>
> (Cf. *Purg.* XIX, 52.)

—and elsewhere Chaucer seems to be mocking Dante: in
the scene in *Purgatorio*, for example, where Dante describes

a golden eagle that came down like a thunderbolt and snatched him up to heaven. Chaucer's eagle in *The House of Fame* is similar but protests at the load it has to carry:

> ...Seynte Marye!
> Thou art noyous for to carye! (ll. 573-4.)

Chaucer's language and style are indeed simpler than Dante's in the sense that they demand less effort of the reader. Chaucer rarely matches the conciseness and precision of the *Comedy*. Dante's method in presenting a character or scene is often to pinpoint a single detail from the many possible, using a minimum of words and leaving much to the reader's imagination. Few English poets have attempted this severity of selection. Chaucer's eagle, mentioned above, is described in much greater detail than Dante's, and Tennyson's Ulysses is a much more talkative man than we find in *Inferno*. Most of the translators find it necessary to elaborate or dilute Dante's cryptic utterances, and some of the poems deriving from Dante sources are unbearably prolix. Leigh Hunt's *Story of Rimini* is an outstanding example. Dante's few lines are expanded into a lengthy poem of four cantos; his art of leaving things unsaid quite escapes Hunt, who fills in the details with merciless thoroughness:

> 'May I come in?' said he: it made her start—
> That smiling voice;—she coloured, pressed her heart
> A moment, as for breath, and then with free
> And usual tone said, 'O yes,—certainly.'
>
> (III, 581-4.)

Again it is Eliot who has perhaps best understood and learnt most from Dante in this respect. 'One has learned from the *Inferno* that the greatest poetry can be written with the greatest economy of words,' although he declared modestly, 'In twenty years I have written about a dozen lines in that style successfully.'[1]

In Leigh Hunt's poem as elsewhere a whole plane of Dante's poetry is lost by a distortion of the point of vision. Dante gives us Francesca's story in her own words. She looks back from *Inferno*, resting for a while from the incessant wind of the circle of the lustful, and she recalls the moment of that fateful kiss, knowing the events that followed and the consequences of her action. The reticence of that widely praised line

> Quel giorno più non vi leggemmo avante*
>
> *(Inf. v, 138.)*

is a sign of her modesty and her confusion, and though Hunt recognizes the power of Dante's reticence, his change of person,

> That day *they* read no more...,

sacrifices much of Dante's effect. The same difficulty is met in Chaucer's Ugolino where the whole structure of the episode changes: in the *Inferno* it is Ugolino who tells the story, and an extraordinary vitality results from this report from within the tower:

> Breve pertugio dentro da la muda...
> m'avea mostrato per lo suo forame
> > più lune già...†   *(Inf. xxxiii, 22–6.)*

[1] T. S. Eliot, *Dante* (1929), pp. 35–6.

* 'That day we read no more.'

† 'A small opening within the mew [...] had shown me through its hole several moons....'

Chaucer's report is his own, from outside:

> Litel out of Pize stant a tour...

Thus Chaucer is tempted to explain what Dante leaves unsaid, at the shutting up of the outer door:

> ...ond'io guardai
> nel viso a' mie' figliuoi sanza far motto.*
>
> (*Inf.* XXXIII, 47–8.)

> He herde it wel, but he spak right noght,
> And in his herte anon there fil a thoght
> That they for hunger wolde doone hym dyen.

Yet if some features of Dante's language could not be transplanted, others could, and the vast store of reminiscences recorded by Paget Toynbee is evidence that Dante's example has left its mark on the style of many English writers. What has particularly impressed English poets of different ages has been Dante's imagery. Dante's supernatural world which could have seemed so remote and unreal, and his scientific, philosophical and moral digressions, which could have been so tedious, are given a vitality and relevance to our experience by a highly imaginative style which uses simile and metaphor as links between the real world of Dante the man and his readers and the fictitious other-world of the poet. The remarkable effectiveness of Dante's similes has been observed by many critics, by Coleridge for example who quoted Dante's simile comparing the revival of his own spirits by Virgil to that of the drooping flowers in the sun's rays:

* '...whereat I looked in the faces of my sons without saying a word.'

Quali i fioretti, dal notturno gelo
  chinati e chiusi, poi che'l sol li 'mbianca
  si drizzan tutti aperti in loro stelo...★

(Inf. II, 127–9.)

—a Virgilian reminiscence, also in Boccaccio, and taken
up by Chaucer in *Troilus and Criseyde*:

But right as floures, thorugh the cold of nyght
Iclosed, stoupen on hire stalke lowe,
Redressen hem ayein the sonne bright...

(II, 967–9.)

Several of Chaucer's Dante reminiscences reveal his
interest in Dante's frequent mingling of abstract and
concrete in various stylistic devices—compare the opening
lines of *Purgatorio*, where Dante likens his treatment of new
material to a boat sailing in calmer waters:

Per correr migliori acque alza le vele
  omai la navicella del mio ingegno...†

(Purg. I, 1–2.)

with Chaucer's lines in *Troilus and Criseyde*:

Owt of thise blake wawes for to saylle,
  O wynd, o wynd, the weder gynneth clere...

(II, 1–2.)

Dante glides backwards and forwards between meta-
phorical and literal meanings with effortless ease, but
Chaucer feels here that a note of explanation is required:

This see clepe I the tempestous matere
  Of disespeir that Troilus was inne... (II, 5–6.)

★ 'Just as little flowers, bent down and closed by the chill of night,
when the sun lights them up stand up quite open on their stems.'

† 'To speed over better waters the little boat of my wit now hoists
her sails.'

Many of the Dante reminiscences in Milton are of similar images:[1] Uriel in *Paradise Lost* gliding down like a shooting star, the sun's orb shining with radiant light 'as glowing iron with fire', the radiance of Raphael's appearance that 'seems another Morn ris'n on mid-morn', the victims of bad priests ('pecorelle... pasciute di vento' (*Par.* XXIX, 106–7; cf. *Ep.* VII, 7)) in *Lycidas*:

> The hungry sheep look up and are not fed
>> But swoln with wind and the rank mist they draw,
>> Rot inwardly and feel contagion spread.

And Milton too has that use of vivid and unusual personification, sometimes close to Dante—Paradise 'smiling', and the sun 'silent as the Moon'.

It was this device that inspired Gray's

> The curfew tolls the knell of parting day

taken from *Purgatorio*:

> ...se ode squilla di lontano
> che paia il giorno pianger che si more★
>>>> (*Purg.* VIII, 5–6.)

—and it certainly attracted Shelley, who declared his indebtedness in the Preface to *Prometheus Unbound*:

The imagery which I have employed in this poem will be found in many instances to have been drawn from the operations of the human mind, or from those external actions by which they are expressed. This is unusual in modern poetry although Dante and Shakespeare are full of instances of the same kind: Dante indeed more than any other poet, and with greater success.

---

[1] For a list of possible Dante reminiscences in *Paradise Lost* see Toynbee, *op. cit.* I, 127.

★ '...if he hears far off the bell that seems to weep for the dying day.'

I do not know exactly what Shelley meant by imagery drawn from the operations of the mind, but there are obvious similarities between Shelley's style in *Prometheus* and Dante's—in the use of allegory and symbolism to represent the intangibles with which the poets are concerned, in the construction of imaginative representations of the physical world to illustrate current scientific and philosophical theory, and in the frequent use of stylistic devices in which mental or spiritual and material phenomena are effectively mingled: wings that are 'swift as thought', fire and snow kneaded together with 'liquid love', etc.—like the air in the *Comedy* 'fearing' the lion, and the rose of Paradise 'germinated' by love. Shelley could find this elsewhere, of course, in classical poets or the metaphysicals, but it is interesting that he alludes specifically to Dante.

This use by Dante of imagery to convey the spiritual in terms of the physical deeply impressed Pound: 'It is expedient in reading the *Commedia*', he wrote, 'to regard Dante's description of the actions and conditions of the shades as descriptions of men's mental states in life, in which they are, after death, compelled to continue: that is to say men's inner selves stand visibly before the eyes of Dante's intellect'; and elsewhere 'Dante's precision in both the *Vita Nuova* and in the *Commedia* comes from the attempt to reproduce exactly the thing which has been clearly seen'.[1] Thanks to Pound and Santayana Eliot came to appreciate Dante's ability to 'realize the inapprehensible in visual images', as in a passage he translated from the *Paradiso*:

[1] E. Pound, *Spirit of Romance*, pp. 114, 117.

'Within its depths I saw ingathered, bound by love in one mass, the scattered leaves of the universe; substance and accidents and their relations, as though together fused, so that what I speak of is one simple flame.'[1] So Eliot explores and extends Dante's symbols, flame and fire, rose and wood:

> In the middle, not only in the middle of the way
> But all the way, in a dark wood, in a bramble,
> On the edge of a grimpen, where is no secure foot-hold,
> And menaced by monsters, fancy lights,
> Risking enchantment.   (*East Coker*, II.)

Here then is one aspect of Dante's art that has been widely acknowledged and appreciated in this country.

While Dante's imagery has survived its journey across the Channel, his metre was never successfully acclimatized here. There is not time now to trace the story of *terza rima* in England, nor would it be entirely appropriate as English readers met this form in other Italian poets too. Although, as we have seen, the early translators shirked the *terza rima*, there were many scattered attempts at this metre by English poets, from Chaucer, Wyatt, Surrey, Harington and Milton to Hayley, Byron, Hunt, Shelley and others, many of them indeed inspired by Dante. Most of these experiments were soon forgotten—Byron in using *terza rima* for his *Prophecy of Dante* thought that this was the first attempt in English literature, apart from Hayley. Shelley was certainly the most successful in this form, which he used, not only in his translations, but also in *The Woodman and the Nightingale*, *The Tower of Famine*, as well as in the

[1] T. S. Eliot, *Dante* (1929), p. 54. Cf. *Par.* XXXIII, 85–90.

Ode to the West Wind, where he groups his tercets in sections of four and concludes each section with a rhyming couplet, which thus seals off what is a fourteen-line stanza. But his most impressive use of this metre is in *The Triumph of Life*, where he handles the tercet with great flexibility, breaking up the rhythm with frequent enjambement and unusual caesuras which tone down the effect of the masculine rhymes and provide considerable dramatic effect. Dante had set the example of breaking the normal pattern of his tercets with bold enjambement and the cut and thrust of rapid dialogue. Shelley goes further:

> But not the less with impotence of will
> They wheel—though ghastly shadows interpose
> Round them and round each other—and fulfil
> Their work, and in the dust from whence they rose
> Sink, and corruption veils them as they lie.
>
> (ll. 170–4.)

Since Shelley a number of poets have attempted to reproduce the pattern of Dante's tercets—Laurence Binyon, for example, who used rhyme but toned down its prominence by various means, using imperfect rhymes, rhyming on an unstressed syllable, or placing a heavy or emphatic syllable before the final word. Pound encouraged him in this, praising his attention to 'the original *sound* as a whole. His "past, admits, checked, kings", all masculine endings, but all leaving a residue of vowel sound in state of potential or latent, as considered by Dante himself in his remarks on troubador verse.'[1]

Another outstanding attempt to master *terza rima* was

---

[1] E. Pound, *Literary Essays* (1954), p. 205.

made by Eliot in *Little Gidding*; here in a passage of seventy-two lines Eliot struggled to find 'an approximation to *terza rima* without rhyming'. He explained later his difficulty: the obtrusiveness of rhyme in English, and the 'shifts and twists' of translators who attempt to reproduce it. 'I therefore adopted for my purpose a simple alteration of unrhymed masculine and feminine terminations as the nearest way of giving the light effect of the rhyme in Italian:

> In the uncertain hour before the morning
>   Near the ending of interminable night
>   At the recurrent end of the unending
> After the dark dove with the flickering tongue
>   Had passed below the horizon of his homing
>   While the dead leaves still rattled on like tin....'

'This section of a poem,' Eliot said, 'not the length of one canto of the *Divine Comedy*, cost me far more time and trouble and vexation than any passage of the same length that I have ever written.'[1]

In this short survey much has had to be omitted and I can only refer briefly to the significance of the *Comedy* for the conception and structure of a number of English poems which must have been written with Dante's example in mind. J. A. W. Bennett has shown the similarities in structure between the *Comedy* and Chaucer's *Parlement of Foules*. Other critics have pointed out Dante's significance in the tradition of the poet-pilgrim device, the 'fallible first-person singular'; the fruitfulness of Dante's technique

[1] T. S. Eliot, 'Talk on Dante', *Kenyon Review* (spring, 1953). See M. Praz, 'T. S. Eliot and Dante', *Eliot, a Selected Critique*, ed. Unger (New York, 1948).

of portraying and commenting implicitly and explicitly
on himself cannot have escaped Chaucer as he wrote the
Canterbury Tales.[1] Would Milton have had the same
grandiose conception without Dante's example before
him? And in the nineteenth century one could point to
Keats's *Fall of Hyperion, a Dream,* which is structurally
close to the *Purgatorio,* and very probably influenced by
Cary's translation of the *Comedy*;[2] or to Tennyson's *In
Memoriam,* of which the author wrote: 'It begins with
death and ends in promise of a new life—a sort of *Divine
Comedy,* cheerful at the close.'[3]

Dante's significance for English letters can never
properly be measured. Quite as important as the various
specific contributions that we have examined was the
simple fact that he *was* Dante, that someone in the distant
past had set the highest standards of artistry and principle
and had left a poem against which subsequent generations
of poets could measure their ideals and achievements.
Many English critics have seen this and have helped to keep
Dante's example before writers and readers in this country
—Shelley for example in his praise of Dante's art: 'His
very words are instinct with spirit; each is a spark, a burn-
ing atom of inextinguishable thought';[4] and William
Godwin in his tribute to Dante's humanity: 'Dante
exhibits powers of which we did not know before that the

[1] See A. L. Kellogg, 'Chaucer's Self-portrait and Dante's', *Medium
Aevum* (1960).

[2] See R. V. W. Gittings, *The Mask of Keats* (1956).

[3] See F. St J. Thackeray, 'Dante and Tennyson', *Temple Bar,* CII,
387–97.

[4] P. B. Shelley, *Works* (1926), VII, 112, 131–2.

heart of man was susceptible, and which teach us to consider our nature as something greater and more astonishing than we had ever been accustomed to conceive it.'[1] That achievement we have commemorated here.

[1] W. Godwin, *Life of Chaucer* (1804), I, 359–60.

DATE DUE